Trials and Triumphs of Following Jesus

BY

Nick Farone

The contents of this work, including, but not limited to, the accuracy of events, people, and places depicted; opinions expressed; permission to use previously published materials included; and any advice given or actions advocated are solely the responsibility of the author, who assumes all liability for said work and indemnifies the publisher against any claims stemming from publication of the work.

Dorrance Publishing Co
585 Alpha Drive
Pittsburgh, PA 15238
Visit our website at *www.dorrancebookstore.com*

ISBN: 978-1-4809-4221-9
eISBN: 978-1-4809-4198-4

Acclaims

"Never in my 54 years of personal ministry and living in a minister's home all my life, have I run across a man like Nick Farone with such blind faith as he and his wife Sandy have. He has the ability to share that kind of faith in every service where he ministers. He carries that same blind faith in Christ Jesus in his daily walk."

Rev. Julius Roberts
Pastor of 43 years Church of God
Hall of Prophets Notable
Cleveland, TN

. . .

"A man of Christian character, devotion, and sincerity, His work with the youth of Louisiana, has been stellar and should serve as a model school. Nick is an awesome husband and father, but I'm most grateful that he's a true friend. Nick's life story is a panoramic view of a man's faith that was literally sculptured by the hands of God."

Pastor Charles A. Istre
Senior Pastor
Living Springs Family Worship Center
Branford, FL

. . .

"This is an extraordinary story of how a man who enjoyed a life of material riches, great comfort and acclaim, gave it all up. It began when he felt a void in his heart and began reaching out to find God. His wonderful wife, Sandy, supported him in his search. Despite many problems and great deprivations, he kept his faith. This book is truly inspirational in its description of how faith really works."

Dave C. Treen
Former Governor of Louisiana

. . .

"It is one thing to preach about faith; it is another thing to live it. Nick Farone has lived it! From Broadway, to Burbank, to Louisiana, Nick shows us how the trials, tribulations, and testing of the faith journey, will produce the miracles, blessings, and faithfulness of God."

Rev. Mike Reed
President, Lamb Broadcasting
West Monroe, LA

Dedication

I dedicate this book to my grandson, ***Dominick Charles Farone III***. There is no greater gift that I can give to my grandson, born July 7, 2015, than this written testimony to the faithfulness of the One true and living God and Savior, Jesus Christ. I want him to know his grandfather was a blessed man because of God. He has given him a wife who has walked this amazing walk of faith with him. He also gave them a son the world told them they could never have. He blessed our son with a loving wife to walk by his side as fellow servants to His son Jesus Christ. God gave them a life filled with the romance and wonder only God can give. He gave them a son to raise in the knowledge of the goodness of the Lord. Part of that knowledge is the meaning of his name "Dominick," which means "Gift from God."

With the completion of this second book, God has passed His mantel of ministry on to them. My hope is that the true testimonies of His guidance and miracles throughout these written pages will inspire and encourage all who endeavor to read this book from beginning to end. It will prove that even in the darkest times of our lives, He is forever at our side walking us through to victory in His name.

God has prepared an inheritance for our son to pass on to our grandson. That inheritance is a true and exciting walk of faith with Jesus Christ.

> ***"A good man leaves an inheritance to his children's children."* Proverbs 13:22 NKJV**

Me combing Christie's hair

Foreword

"Singing On A Different Stage"
By Rhonda Miskowski

Nick Farone was brushing Christie's hair for an hour, and he'll brush it for an hour more before the photographer, feverishly aiming his lens, gets his shot. The gig will pay him $1,000.

It's not his first time in front of a camera. In college, he ran with Robert Redford in *The Way We Were*. "We were told to make sure we didn't run faster than him—to stay five lengths behind so he would look good. He was a very nice guy—very down to earth," Farone remembers.

Nick Farone is, and always has been, a prolific performer. Acting, singing, modeling—he's a natural. Every entertainment goal he ever set, he met or exceeded. He had everything he wanted…he thought.

Dominick Farone was born into an Italian Catholic home in New York State. His father was a Vaudeville entertainer. His mother, a devout Catholic, died when he was only twelve. Farone shared his father's love of music and studied opera at the Boston Conservatory of Music. After singing in various dinner theaters in Boston, a chance meeting in New York City got him an audition with the famed Beverly Sills, who hired him as her second tenor.

"God will allow us to follow our heart's desires, even when they are not His perfect plan for our lives," says Farone of these turn of events. “He always has a plan *B*. Learning how faith works, however, directs us to His plan A.”

Although unsaved at the time, Farone was hired to sing in the choir of Marble Collegiate Church, where he was impressed and moved by the sermons. “I had heard enough empty preaching in my lifetime. This man was different,” Farone remembers. “He talked about Jesus like he knew Him personally.”

Farone was offered his first TV role—as Salvatore, an Italian cook—in the soap opera *Love of Life*. He went to his pastor for direction, who advised, “Give your life to Jesus. Trust Him—He will direct you.”

Nick accepted the role of Salvatore and went on to play on *All My Children*, *One Life to Live*, *As the World Turns*, and the *Edge of Night*. Soon he was singing in Rodney Dangerfield’s club, the Riverboat, among others. He began picking up TV commercials and was acting in films. For all his fame, something eluded him—peace.

One night after performing at the renowned Concord Hotel in the Catskill Mountains, he bowed following a standing ovation from thousands, and then retreated to his dressing room.

“I felt like my life was pointless. It was the loneliest, emptiest feeling I ever had. I realized that I didn’t really help anybody. Oh, I entertained them for a while made them laugh, made them cry, but I didn’t change anyone’s life for the better. I sat there in my dressing room all by myself, lost and empty.”

Soon after, Farone and his longtime girlfriend, Sandy, went to a Polish Catholic church, where Nick heard God call him by name: “Dominick, I want you to love Me.”

Suddenly, Nick was weeping uncontrollably and asking Jesus into his life.

“What can I do for You, Jesus?” he asked. “Sing,” was the reply.

Farone felt this request was too small and too easy. He asked again, and heard the same reply: “Sing.”

He started singing in churches. He married Sandy. Still, with the changes Jesus made in his life, Nick’s professional career was moving

Me in my Tuxedo poster

forward. California called and they moved. Bigger parts came, producing and starring in theatrical productions, commercials, opera, soap operas, private clubs, and elegant parties. It was his for the taking, and he took.

Although all of Farone's soap-opera characters were positive (doctor, lawyer, police officer), he soon grew convicted. "I realized I was part of an industry that promotes everything that hurts us."

The call came while Nick Farone was standing atop the Beverly Hills Hotel. He was playing a doctor on *General Hospital*—his favorite role. Previously a medic in the Army, the medical lingo came easy to him. Easy role, easy money, comfortable life—too comfortable.

He stood there and looked down at the limousines and fur coats. "My spirit was disquieted as I reviewed in my mind what the world of entertainment had become," he said.

He began contemplating his career. "*Is it worth it—profit achieved at any cost?*" he asked himself.

"Integrity, morals, and principles were thrown out, and now anything was accepted as art," he concluded.

Farone's only comfort was in his singing, but not in the opera or on Broadway. Singing for God's glory alone brought him pure joy. The haunting questions stopped when God's voice once again whispered to him on top of the hotel that night.

"Serve Me full-time," God said. "I knew His voice," said Farone. "I'd heard it before."

Full-time ministry. It was his answer to peace. He went home and told his wife.

"It was her, behind the scenes, diligently praying, that brought me to the feet of Jesus. In the twenty years I spent in the entertainment world living solely for myself, it was no easy walk for her."

Now, it was over. Full-time ministry was calling. Sandy was relieved at her husband's news. It was an answer to prayer.

"I promised God I would serve Him only. Well, the first month we used our rent money to get the ministry started. When rent came due, we sold our TV set to pay it. The second month, we sold our living-room set, and the third month we gave up our health insurance," he recalls.

Farone was getting worried, but God was still talking. "Trust Me," He said.

Trust they did. Farone enrolled in Bible College. The entertainment business, however, did not let him go quietly. Offers continued to pour in. HBO called asking for fifteen minutes of his time for a handsome sum in return. He needed the money but turned them down flat. He turned everyone down. For him, it was all or nothing. He had made a promise to God and he intended to keep it.

Soon, ministry opportunities opened up around the country. Farone sang from church to church. God replaced everything they had given up and more. Sandy, who was told by doctors that she could never have children, gave birth to a son, Dominick Jr.

They settled in Louisiana, where they opened up a center for under-privileged kids. "In 15 years we have reached 2,400 children in a city that has a population of only 11,000 total," he said.

The governor of Louisiana took note and set up a meeting between Farone and President George Bush Sr. The President lauded Farone's work as something that should be duplicated around the country.

Louisiana's a far cry from Hollywood, and Farone confesses there are some perks he misses. But he added, "I don't miss at all the deviant lifestyle that most live in the world of showbiz. People just see all the glamour and money. They don't know what goes on behind the scenes to achieve that kind of success."

Today, Farone is an Ordained Bishop with the Church of God. He and his wife Sandy still travel all over the world ministering in churches. Farone sings, evangelizes, and writes. His testimony is given in his book *Faith How It Works*. He desires to pass on to people everywhere everything God has taught him about leading a lifestyle of faith.

"My family is a living testimony to God's faithfulness to His Word," he declares, referencing Hebrews 11:6 "People will let you down, but there is One who is faithful to His promise. His name is Jesus."

Rhonda Miskowski serves with her husband, Rob, who is youth and discipleship director of the Church of God in Louisiana. **Evangel Magazine *July 2011 Edition***

Preface

I'm sitting here in our stateroom on a ship bound for Hawaii. It is another answer to prayer. Sandy is out on the balcony reading one of her favorite Amish writers. The Pacific is blue and calm with the puffy white clouds reflecting off its waters. We had been looking forward to this trip for ten years, praying and hoping God would send the right people to take over and continue a magnificent work He used us to establish from the ground up. It was no easy calling or task, as is anything in life worth doing, but when God puts a calling, a vision, or a dream in your heart you cannot turn away from it. This book came about as a sequel to my first book, ***Faith How It Works***. Sandy and I have lived a life receiving God's richest blessings by just learning how to trust and follow Him through his Word and stepping out in faith. This book is not about a certain type of "religion" to follow; God knows we have enough of them. It is a book about following a person that you can trust to guide you through life, each and every day, through each and every circumstance you will face, along your life's journey.

It's not written by someone who speculates what will happen if certain daily practices are followed. It is a book written by someone who has walked the talk, to test and prove the One they are following. That One is Jesus. Is it a religious book? Some would call it that if religion is all they know. What it really is about is a relationship with someone you cannot see or touch in the physical sense, but is silently there with you every moment helping and guiding you throughout your life.

Finally, life's journey is filled with trials and triumphs we all face every day. You can't walk through this brief excursion of this planet without facing them. But there is definitely a way to live more victoriously. It all depends on Who you are choosing to follow on your journey.

My first book was read over and over by those who bought it and put its suggestions into a daily practice. Why? Because they saw the positive outcome it brought to their lives. My prayer is that this book will do the same for all of its readers.

In His service,
Bishop Nick Farone

Introduction

Ever since I was a small boy of twelve years old, I always wanted to help people and to somehow make their lives better. I had a father that was an entertainer for most of his life, and I saw how people who went to his performances enjoyed themselves and had a good time as he played the saxophone. He began his career at the age of eighteen in vaudeville. Later in life he had his own trio and played in nightclubs and for weddings and banquets. He even played the musical saw, which really impressed me. He did this until the time when he had to leave performing to take care of his wife, who became bedridden from severe migraine headaches and the medication she took to try and ease her pain. My family consisted of six children, me being the youngest, which necessitated my father taking a job at the local locomotive company in Schenectady, NY, making train parts to provide for his family.

I remember my dad coming home from work each day and collapsing into his chair in front of our TV set. He would turn it on and watch a man by the name of Red Skelton do routines that would make my dad laugh or sometimes cry. As he did I would watch and see the pressures of the day released from his face. "That's what I want to do," I would exclaim to my four sisters and brother. I saw how this man did truly help people just by entertaining them for an hour.

This being said, I went into the entertainment world to fulfill my heart's desire to touch people through singing and acting. I did pretty well, but I realized that I really didn't help change anyone's life for the better. I was left with an emptiness I felt I couldn't fill in my life.

After I came to the realization that the only One who could really change a person's life was Jesus Christ, I gave my heart to Him and let Him guide me from that day forward.

Reading the Bible one day I came across a challenge Jesus made to a rich young ruler in **Matthew 19: 16-22: "*Go sell what you have and give to the poor, and you will have treasure in heaven; and come follow Me,*" NKJV**. A challenge he declined, but I decided to accept. That story is told in my first book, ***Faith How it Works***.

For the past thirty-seven years we have lived the most exciting and amazing life anyone could hope to live and seen the impossible become possible. "How?" you ask. By believing and trusting God to keep His promises written in the Bible.

This book will prove to you that in the greatest trials you will face in your life, if you believe God and *do not give up*, you can see victory. The scripture promises; Trust, Delight, and Commit *will* come true in your life as well.

***"Trust in the Lord, and do good; Dwell in the land and feed on His faithfulness. Delight yourself in the Lord and He shall give you the desires of your heart. Commit your way to the Lord, Trust also in Him, and He shall bring it to pass."* Psalm 37:3-5 NKJV**

Chapter One (Trial)

***"For with God nothing will be impossible"* Luke 1:37 NKJV**

It was Easter Sunday 1994, and word had gotten out that we had scheduled an *Easter Sunrise Service* at our home in Louisiana. Those who didn't have a church to go to that Sunday were invited by word of mouth. We told a few friends service would be at 7:00 A.M. and it would be just a simple service with communion.

Bang, bang, bang! "Nick, someone is banging on our back door," Sandy said. "You're dreaming, it's only 4:30 A.M. and it's still dark out, go back to sleep," I said. Bang, bang, bang, bang, bang! "Okay, I hear it now, I'll check it out." We lived off the road about 300 yards back in the woods, and even though we had regular visitors of the raccoon persuasion, this was much more determined than they were. Grabbing my PR24 baton I had kept from my security days in years past, I slowly walked up to the back door window and peeked out.

There stood a family of folks I had never seen before. A man, a woman, two boys, a younger woman, and another man were all peeking in the back door window. I quickly put my weapon away and opened the door.

"Can I help you?" I asked "We heard there's a Easter Sunrise Service here and we wanted to attend," the older fellow said. Looking at the clock it was 4:50 A.M. "Yes, there is, but it doesn't start until 7:00 A.M." I said, hoping one of them had a watch and would see the early hour. No such luck. "That's okay, we can wait," the young couple said. Sandy was now up and rounded the corner in her bathrobe. I ushered our visitors into our tiny living room and said, "Ya'll can wait here while I get dressed and put some coffee on." "That'd be fine," the young man said. "Could I have some water for my wife? She's not feeling too good." he continued. "Sure," I said.

As they settled into our living room I heard, "Ut-oh she's not going to make it. Do you have a bathroo…ah… too late… I'm so sorry," the young man said. Then his wife instantly vomited on our carpet. "No problem, get some paper towels, Nick," Sandy said, running over to the young lady. "Okay," I said, rushing into the kitchen and coming back with handfuls of something I think, at that hour, may have been napkins.

We found out later the young woman was expecting her first arrival and was in her early stages of pregnancy. "This will be an Easter we will never forget," I said to Sandy. Boy was that a prophetic understatement, I didn't know I was making at that time. From that moment on, God would take the most unlikely people to do a most extraordinary work in Louisiana. Twenty-three people would begin to change a city.

Chapter Two (Triumph)

"For God so loved the world that He gave His only begotten Son, that whosoever believes in Him should not perish, but have everlasting life." John 3:16 NKJV

From that first Easter Sunday at our home we knew God was up to something new in our lives. It was a lovely service with twenty-three people. Someone made a cross from the ivy vines in our backyard. We hung it up and snuggled together in our sun room to have an intimate sunrise service. Some folks drove all the way from Mississippi to attend, and they made breakfast for all of us. It brought to mind what the early church must have been like meeting in homes.

We sat around just talking afterwards, and these folks asked me to stay and start a church. The city already had 110 churches, with a population of 13,000, and I felt it didn't need another one. I told them they had their pick of churches. Besides, we were already scheduled a year in advance to do services in churches all around the country. They said they wanted to do more than go to church, they wanted to do something special for our Lord. So, I told them I would *pray about it.* Many people say that to keep from doing what they don't want to do and use God as an out, but I really meant it.

"God, it took us a long time to get to this point in our ministry. Why would You ask me to give up the only income we have going to the churches on Sundays? This is crazy! They don't need another church here. What they need is a work for the youth in this city, nobody wants to reach. I know what I'll do, I will give up my services for two months, do my best to reach out to the youth and have the churches here take them into their services. That way these fine folks can attend one of the churches that take the kids in, problem solved," I thought.

Contacting all the pastors in town, I had known for years, the responses were shocking. They all said "*No*." "We don't want those kids in our church." "They are the wrong color for our church." "These are problem kids; we don't want them here with our kids." "They are the wrong denomination for us." The excuses were endless. You know when someone doesn't want to do something they can find all the reasons they can't, very easily.

Back to my knees I went in prayer. It does something when you are on your knees praying. It makes you more focused and alert, I guess. "You do it," God said to me. His voice was now a familiar one in my life. "You do it," He said again.

"Okay, God, I know about fleeces and witnesses, from Your word, so I want *five* witnesses, of my choosing, from You and if You answer all of them I will know this is You. I will leave the road and establish a work here for underprivileged children." That was my pledge. They were big witnesses too, no small challenges to God; after all, He's God! First was a place to meet on Sunday mornings. Second was enough money to be given in the offering to pay each week for the rental of the space. Third, we needed enough money to be sent in by our Prayer Partners so we could eat and pay our own bills. Fourth, I wanted my own weekly newspaper article to let people know what we were doing. Finally, the big one, number five, I didn't think could possibly happen. I wanted my own Christian TV program on the local station to get the Word out.

Chapter Three (Triumph)

"Now faith is the substance of things hoped for the evidence of things not seen." Hebrews 11:1 NKJV

The first witness God gave was to give us the most expensive place in the city to meet, the Municipal Center. Not one of the churches in town would allow me to use one of their buildings, they were not using, on Sunday to meet for two hours. So what did God do? The city rented me their Municipal Center Building for $325.00 for three hours on Sunday morning. I thought, "Okay, God, this will be the shortest run for services in this city."

That first Sunday twenty people showed up in this huge building. We set up chairs, sound equipment, worshiped, prayed, and the people gave $330.00 in the offering. I laughed, God even gave $5.00 extra for me and my family that Sunday. This was amazing!

We started meeting regularly, after that first Sunday at the Municipal Center. Our adult numbers started to grow. We never missed paying $325.00 a week for the three hours we were allowed to use the Center. However, we knew if we were going to make a difference in the city, we needed our own place.

Word started to spread that an ex-TV actor was holding services in town. One Baptist preacher started saying. "We got one of them tongue talkers here." That's another name for Pentecostal Preacher.

For those of you who are not preacher talk savvy, that means I am baptized in the Holy Spirit with evidence of speaking in a heavenly language. I am not ashamed of it, nor do I impose His will on other people. It is my strength and the power He gives me to accomplish the impossible. Without it, I would never have been able to establish this magnificent work for children, in a city filled with all kinds of racial, spiritual, and religious prejudice. I would not be able to write this book to encourage you today to believe God for the impossible.

The editor of the local newspaper asked me if I would like to write a weekly article in the "Religious" section. A friend of mine, who owned his own Christian TV Station, gave me my own TV program called *New Beginnings*. We even had our own theme song called, "It's a New Beginning." Our personal income we received from our traveling Sunday services was gone now, but God started touching our Prayer Partners around the country to send in enough each month to pay our personal bills like, electric, water, food, clothing, insurance for our car. In three months God was giving us the witnesses we had asked for. Now we needed our own place.

It was the end of June, and I was walking around the worst neighborhood in town praying. This is where I would see twelve-year-old girls, at night, standing outside one of the worst bars in town, with babies on their hips. I asked myself, "Where would Jesus go if He were trying to reach the lost youth of this city?" A clear inner voice said, "Here."

Turning around I saw two empty buildings. There was no "rent" or "for sale" sign on them, so I thought, I didn't hear right. But that voice was so clear I was inspired to contact the man who owned the buildings. Tracking him down I realized he was not a real follower of Jesus, if you know what I mean. However, he was looking to make a profit. "I want $750.00 a month to rent them," he said, looking down his nose at me. I said to him, "Look, I work with kids, I have no money to work with, but if you will allow me to have these broken down, rat-infested buildings, *rent free for two years*, I will make all the improvements and pay for them myself."

God will give you the boldness only He can give when He sees your heart and it goes along with His will. You just have to have the faith to step out and I did. I think I saw little dollar sign lights flash in this man's eyes and he said, "Okay," and with a handshake we agreed.

On July 4, 1994, we had our own place and God had given me all five witnesses I had asked for.

Old storefront and inside room July 4, 1994

First Sanctuary

Celebrate Jesus Banner

Chapter Four (Triumph)

"For whoever has, to him more will be given, and he will have abundance." Matthew 13:12 NKJV

As the weeks progressed, our little place started to take shape. We got the rats out first thing. "Nick, Nick, come quick, I got one under my broom!" George shouted. Sure enough, I left painting the wall, with paintbrush still in hand, to assist in the "Battle of the Rat" with George, and the rat, the size of a Chihuahua, lost. We plugged the hole he came in, between the wall and outdoors.

Friends we had from Mississippi now lived in Louisiana and started driving eighty-five miles, one way, to have services with us and help.

The TV program was making people aware of what we were doing and they wanted to help. My small sound system I ministered with around the country fit perfect in our little sanctuary. We also wanted to have some live music to worship before service. George had a beat-up old snare drum with the skinhead held together by masking tape. We used some salad forks we had as drums sticks, which sounded pretty good. A family from the city where I had my TV program started coming to service, and their daughter Melissa brought and played her electric keyboard. It had no piano stand, so the top of a garbage can worked nicely.

We rounded up some old metal chairs, and George made some kneelers for an altar out of an old pool table he had. Our son Nicky's old diaper changing table became my first pulpit. The cross, made out of vines for our first service at our home, worked perfect on the fake wall we made. Someone gave us some plants to hang on both sides of the cross, and I made a banner that read, "***Everybody is Somebody in the Body***."

The pastors in town started to avoid us, and we didn't understand why. Our little place was God's church in action. People were working together for the betterment of those less fortunate.

Chapter Five (Triumph)

"That your charitable deed may be in secret; and your Father, who sees in secret, will Himself reward you openly." Matthew 6:4 NKJV

Weeks passed, and our numbers continued to grow. New kids started showing up each week. A front page article in the local newspaper brought in more adults who wanted to do something more for God than just attend a church on Sunday.

"Rev. Nick Farone's vision to bring in youth off the street and give them a wholesome environment is right on the money," the publisher of the local newspaper wrote.

We had a car wash to raise money for some games for the future Youth Center. I made sandwich board signs and hung them around my neck. Then I walked around the streets attracting attention. Seventy people brought their cars, and we raised $400.00 That provided for the purchase of three used video games, rental of two pool tables, and we built a ping pong table out of a piece of plywood and some two-by-fours.

Friends of ours in Mississippi gave us some used candy vending machines from their business, and we rented some soda machines from a distributor in a nearby city. Friends in California, who were getting some new office furniture, sent us their old office furniture for our Center. It estimated at about $4,000.00.

Each week articles would be written about us in our local paper. The TV program was also being well received, and people started to send in support. In one year, we had 275 kids signed up at our Youth Center. It was incredible to see how our faith was being honored by God. Most of the churches in the city were still against us, but we had two start to support us in our work.

It is true when God starts to bless, others will be jealous, although they won't say it out loud. People will just quietly voice their opinions to each other in their various denominational houses. Pastors won't do or say anything negative about you, so it gives the appearance they are not against you, but the assurance that you won't hurt their church.

"Nick Farone, by God's calling, has come to this community to minister and to bring the Good News to these people. Reverend Farone is not called here to steal sheep from other churches. There is no contradiction that our community needs such a non-denominational missionary," one writer wrote to the editor.

God was doing His best to reach His underprivileged children. By October of 1994, we were seeing many of the Youth in our community coming to the Center for special functions. The churches said the children would be allowed to come to our Center's functions as long as they didn't interfere with the programs at their home church. We had 175 attend our Harvest Party instead of "trick-or-treating" in October.

Chapter Six (Trial)

"Let your light so shine before men, that they may see your good works, and glorify your Father in heaven." Matthew 5:16 NKJV

Now I would have to raise more and more funds as the Center continued to grow. Ninety percent of the support for *New Beginnings* came from outside the city. I kept singing and preaching in the churches around the country that had been so supportive of us all these years. This time, however, I would tell them what we were doing and allow God to use them to help His kids. They were always very generous, but the traveling and working at the center began to take its toll.

Returning from one of these fundraising trips, I was eager to do Sunday Service again at our place. Rushing in the door to get to my pulpit for Sunday's message, I saw a new figure sitting in the last row, by the back door. I had entered so quickly I walked right past him.

He was a young man, about seventeen years old, around six foot, one inches tall, and a solid 180 pounds. He sat slouched in the back chair with his head facing the floor, right leg stretched out with the left leg tucked under it. As I approached him, I noticed some tattoos and dirty words cut into his arm. Not by a professional, but by a sheet rock knife I later learned he carried as a weapon. Walking up to him I said,

"Good morning, I'm Pastor Nick," the young man didn't even look up. He just sat there with his right hand resting on his knee, palm down. "Well, I just want you to know I'm happy you're here and I hope you enjoy the service," still no response. I left quietly and walked back to the pulpit.

After service, I saw this young man get up and leave before anyone could talk to him. Each week it was the same thing. "Good morning, I'm so happy you're here, I hope you enjoy the service," still no response. He'd sit in the same seat, with the same posture, every week, and depart quickly after service was over.

I found out from some of the other kids he was one of the gang leaders. He had a brother that was in prison, another brother that was in a gang, a little brother who wanted to be in a gang, and a mother who was an alcoholic. His father was nowhere to be found. When he stood up, he was menacing. His six foot one, solid muscle frame, and dark African American completion made him a formidable threat. He had eyes that held the cold emptiness of a shark when he looked up long enough for you to look in them.

After a month or so, my persistence each Sunday paid off. "Good morning, I'm so happy you are here," I said and stretched out my hand as usual. This time my outstretched hand was met with an upturned right hand. It still rested on his knee though. He turned his hand upward so I could shake hands with his fingers. I didn't know what to do. I was caught off guard, so I stood there shaking his fingers for a few moments then proceeded to the pulpit for Sunday's message. He still slipped away quickly after the service, but that was okay, we had made contact. Little by little each week he started to look up a bit and actually shook my hand with a full handshake as the weeks passed.

Now, there is a soft side to this ministry. My wife, Sandy, has a special way about her. She began to reach out to this young man each Sunday, as she did to all the kids who came. She would give her gracious greeting to him, but where I got no verbal response, Sandy would get some barely audible response from him. One Sunday she said, "Would you do me a favor? Would you speak up for me? Because what you have to say is important and I want to be able to hear you." From that Sunday on he would speak so we could hear him. Not many words, but the ones he said we could hear. He even moved up closer to the front of the room for service and lingered a bit afterwards. What a great feeling it is to see God transforming a life before your eyes.

Things were moving right along. Some kids were becoming regulars. Some of their moms or guardians would even come to a service once in a while, just to check out the white people their kids were talking about. We even had a makeshift kitchen now behind the fake wall we had built. We started "Pizza Night" on Fridays, at the Youth Center, to get the kids off the streets. The local pizza place gave us a break on the cost of pizzas. Sometimes I'd buy twenty or so. I remember we had to make sure each child got two pieces so we numbered their plates, otherwise some kids would jam whole slices in their mouths at a time and try to get six or seven pieces. Keep in mind these kids got nothing at home, especially pizza, and they were taught "everyone for themselves."

It was great work—hard work, but great work! It takes time to change a lifestyle, so you had to expect setbacks, but this one really blew my mind.

Chapter Seven (Trial)

"No weapon formed against you shall prosper..."
Isaiah 54:17 NKJV

With the type of children God was sending us, a normal day of refereeing fights was the routine. I'd have to break up fights or defuse verbal confrontations on a regular basis. That's what these kids were taught by example in the households they lived in. The toughest was in control.

One young boy, who was only ten years old, would always be the first one at church or any event we had. He lived just down the street with his brother, who weighed 400 pounds. Whenever we had events that awarded prizes, this young man would win and take the prize home to show it off. His brother would take it away from him, play with it, and break it, as a show of power and control. Customarily our little guy would let him or suffer the consequences. One of the consequences was his 400-pound brother would run, if you can picture that, and jump on him with all his weight. To this day I don't know how he survived these sumo wrestler attacks without broken bones or crushed body parts. God's protection is the only explanation.

Now you get the picture about a normal day for us at the Center. Sandy would work with the girls, who were just as tough as the boys, and I with the boys.

With Thanksgiving coming up I wanted to do something special for the adults and youth at the Center. I had prepared a Thanksgiving message and told the kids to invite their families. It would be a day of feasting. If you want people to attend an event, offer them food.

Things were going great. Thirty-eight people responded, and twenty of them were adults. Some of them had never been to the Center with their kids. It was an awesome day. Not one fight or dispute to break up. People seemed to enjoy the message, and the food was wonderful. We had turkey, ham, and all the fixings. Yeah! I was ecstatic. What a wonderful Thanksgiving day. It would be one to remember. That's for sure!

After the festivities we were in our makeshift kitchen doing dishes and rejoicing when one of the youth, I don't remember which, came running in and said, "Pastor Nick, come quick, so-and-so's got a knife and he's slashing the tires on our bikes!" "Oh, God now what?" I said.

Running out front I saw our six-foot young man standing there holding a six-inch switchblade, like a statue, pointing it at me. When I approached him, I saw the anger in his eyes and he didn't move. Looking him square in the eye, I said, "Give me the knife," as calm as I could be. He stood his ground as if challenging me. Once again I said, "Give me the knife," a little firmer. He still didn't move. Then a holy boldness entered me or maybe my old Sicilian nature flared up, I don't know which, but I said, "IF YOU WANT TO STICK SOMETHING, STICK ME OR GIVE ME THE KNIFE!"

Slowly he closed the blade and handed me the knife. Now that the basic threat was over, I was able to speak my mind. "Are you crazy? What is wrong with you? Why did you do this?" He had slashed the tires on ten bikes.

"They made fun of me," he mumbled. "They made fun of you?" I said. "Listen to me, you could be a Youth Leader here some day, instead of a gang leader. God can use you because these kids look up to you. Now you have taught them if somebody does something to them they don't like, pull out a knife and slash something or someone." He hung his head. I continued, "You've got to make this right," I said. "I want you to measure each tire you slashed and buy new tubes for each one to show these kids you made a mistake and want to make it right." Our young man had a small part-time job at the Vo-tech School cleaning up, and he made about $124.00 a week, take-home pay, and he would give his check to his mother. At that moment he just turned and walked away from me. When I went to go after him, he turned sharply and came toward me in a confrontation mode. I braced myself to be hit by a 180 pound right cross. "Oh boy, lights out for Pastor Nick," I thought.

He got right in my face and said, "Mr. Nick, can you meet me here tomorrow morning and take me to Wal-Mart so I can buy the tubes?" That was unexpected. "I sure can," I said. "And I want you to know I am proud of you," I continued. Then he just turned and walked away.

Bright an early the next morning we met at the Center and I took him to Wal-Mart. He wanted to buy new tubes *and tires*, because he said he ruined them both. It cost him $123.00 from his $124.00 paycheck.

Back to the Center we went and word had already spread to the kids who had their tires slashed, so they were there waiting. Let me tell you, it was like Christmas for these kids. Most of the tires they had were already bald with areas you could actually see the tube protruding. One by one we replaced each tire and tube. I found out this young man was quite a hard worker.

"Listen, you guys," I said. "A mistake was made yesterday, and he has made it right today and blessed you, as a way of saying he's sorry. Now you need to say you're sorry for making fun of him."

"I'm sorry," came the first response. "Yeah, me too I'm sorry." One by one, they all thanked him and said they were sorry. I saw a real change in that once hardened young man that day. I saw a softness enter those cold eyes, for the first time. This was the beginning of a real changed life for him, as the months ahead would prove.

Chapter Eight (Trial)

"And the King will answer and say to them, Assuredly, I say to you, inasmuch as you did it to one of the least of these My brethren, you did it to Me." Matthew 25:40 NKJV

Many of our kids wanted to come to church, but didn't have a way there. Most churches with money and a congregation have church vans to pick up the youth and elderly; that's what we needed. "Let's see," I said: $23,000.00 for a new van and $300.00 in our account, hummm. God, Your word says, "He who is faithful with little will be given much," so what can I get with $300.00?

Looking around town I found an old van, with no motor, I could have for $300.00. I figured I had to start somewhere, so I bought the van with no motor. A friend who had an auto repair shop said he would find me a used motor for $360.00 and put it in for us.

In a couple of weeks, he had done just that, and I had raised the $360.00. We were so excited I thought I'd take it on a test run to Natchez, MS, to share the good news with some friends.

About twenty-three miles from Natchez, in Vidalia, LA, smoke started coming out the back of the van and we pulled into a Pizza Hut. We found that one of the mechanics didn't tighten the valve covers down and oil had leaked out all over the motor. Not a good thing!

We had to leave the van in Vidalia for four months waiting for another motor. Finally, after raising the money, spending another $1,000 on another motor, we had our van back ready to pick up the kids on Sunday. It still cost less than a new one and we used what we had. We named the van "Job."

One of the things I knew would really teach these children life's values would be to show them how they could be a blessing to someone else who had less than they did. From their perspective, in their world, everybody had more than they did, so that would be a hard sell. "Bong!" "Light Bulb." "Take them to Mexico on a Missions trip," popped into my head.

I knew a person who took Missions trips in his RV to Mier and Progresso, Mexico. He would stay just across the border in Rio Grande, Texas, at a Mission facility, and go back and forth in vans. I contacted him and asked if he would take a group of us adults and kids with him. He said sure, that would be fine.

So we planned our first Missions trip for that following July. Yeah, I know, in the heat of the summer, but that's when they were going, so we made our plans.

For those of you who have never taken a Mission trip, when you go to the places we were going to, they do not have much of anything. The food you bring has to be basic. They have no running water or refrigeration. Rice, beans, flour, and candy for the children are what we would bring. We decided to bring bottled water to hand out as well. Most there have no electricity. One town is made up of cardboard box houses. Some had wire fence strands around them to show that particular space was a person's home.

The streets are dirt and filled with holes, so you had to drive slowly. Some of our adults brought boxes of Corn Flakes and Cheerios to give away. Not thinking these folks had no milk or place to keep it. It would be a real eye-opening experience for the adults as well as for the kids.

We raised 1,000 pounds of rice, beans, and flour plus some water, candy, and little toys to give to the children. One lady brought a bunch of old Barbie dolls she had, to give to the girls. Off we went in "Job" and our Ram Charger we had traveled the country in for the past seven years.

Eight adults and ten wide-eyed kids drove up to the mission house in Texas, run and owned by two ex-Hell's Angels members. It was a three-story white house, right off the highway. Behind it were bunkhouses they had built, over the years, to house weekend mission-minded people.

They had air-conditioning in each building and communal bathrooms outside. You had to bring your own bedding and food, but mattresses were provided. Six dollars per person, per day, was the charge to cover the cost of electric and water consumption. They had a storage house and two fifteen-passenger vans they took stuff into Mexico with each day. That meant we didn't have to drive our vehicles into Mexico. We could leave them at the mission.

Tired from the long drive, we got settled in to our bunkhouses and planned to eat and rest up for the next day. There were signs posted all around that read, "Beware of rattlesnakes and scorpions." That would make it real fun going to the bathroom in the middle of the night. Another fun thing was the stories the missionary would tell around the campfire just before retiring for the night.

Remember I said they were both ex-Hell's Angels members? They were truly a testimony of how Jesus can change a life, once it is given to Him. Even though they were now serving our Lord, the courage they had to face anything in life never left them. Many people think giving your life to Christ makes you weak. Not true!

Sitting by the campfire, the owner of the facility pulled out a ten-inch-blade Bowie knife he carries with him at all times. "See this handle," he said pointing to a large silver knob at the base of his knife. "When we saw this house we knew it would be perfect for what we wanted to do with the rest of our lives. Stay here and build a mission to take people into Mexico to minister to the poor people. We got the house for real cheap, because it was haunted. No one wanted to live in it," he said.

"That didn't scare us, so we bought it and moved right in. The first night we heard something like a ghost crawling around, but couldn't tell where it was coming from, so we ignored it and went to sleep. The second night she," pointing to his wife, "woke me up and said, 'I think the ghost is in the walls, I can hear it moving around in there.'

"Sure enough, I went over to our bedroom wall and I could hear it inside. I got this knife right here and I was going to let the ghost know, I mean business, this is our house now," he said. "I told it to get out and slammed this handle right through the wall. Then I got the surprise of my life. Hundreds of rattlesnakes started pouring out of that hole. We made a bee-line out of the bedroom, down the stairs, and out of the house. The next day we called an exterminator and had them all taken out. We thank God for them snakes. That's why we got the house so cheap. Those little buggers were the ghosts everyone was afraid of, ain't God good," he concluded with such glee. After that story we all went to bed in our bunkhouses, but I don't think any of us slept.

Chapter Nine (Triumph)

And the King will answer and say to them, "Assuredly, I say to you, inasmuch as you did it to one of the least of these My brethren, you did it to Me." Matthew 25:40 NKJV

The next morning we were up bright and early, loading up the vans with all the stuff we brought to take into Mexico. One of the other things that was asked of the visiting missionary folks was to help them with anything they needed done around the mission.

I mentioned earlier that our young Youth Leader in training was a real good worker. He went with us on this trip to help. There was a big old tree in the back of the mission house that needed pruning. He offered to stay behind and prune the tree for them. He would miss going into Mexico with us this day, but I could see he had a heart to help doing something for the Mission. Staying behind he began working with a little hand saw because that's all they had. The rest of us loaded up and headed out.

This would be our day of mission work and tomorrow would just be a fun day. The missionary would take us across the border to one of the Mexican restaurants to eat some real Mexican food before we headed back home. The kids could buy some souvenirs with the money we gave them.

When you go across the border, you are taking your chances. You never know if you will get a good border patrol guard on the Mexican side or not. A good one will just pass you on through and a bad one will confiscate anything they see they want.

The trick is to hide, as best you can, what you are bringing in to give to the poor. Our sound system we brought with us to sing at the orphanage covered a lot of the food and toys. The kids sat on the rest hoping the guards would not ask them to move. It's a chance you have to take. Being the missionaries made daily trips, most of the guards knew them and knew they were helping the poor. They usually let them go right through without a problem. However, there was always the chance you'd get a "newbie" guard.

Approaching the border we were all a little nervous. This was the first time for most of us. I told you our missionaries were fearless. We pulled into the border crossing and the guard gave us the customary once over, but we heard our missionary guide start to get upset. Speaking something to him in Spanish she said, "Just because we are Americans you think you can overcharge us. This is outrageous!"

All of a sudden there we were, pulled over to the side by two guards and told to wait. Her husband had already made it across the border in the other van, so we thought we were on our way to a Mexican jail. A few minutes later, as we were sitting there praying, we saw the friendly face of her husband come walking back across the border and up to the guardhouse. His wife was still miffed, but her husband and a few American dollars to the guard got us all moving again. I had heard what Mexican jails were like, and I am glad we didn't have to experience them firsthand.

"Whew! That was a close one," I said. "We shouldn't have paid them," she said and resolved to just accept it.

Driving a ways into the city, we stopped at the local doctor's office to drop off some supplies we had brought with us. Not like any office we are used to going to in the states. It was a shabby two-room apartment. A shower curtain separated the two rooms, which indicated one was for examining and the other for operating. That was an eye-opening experience for me to see how poor these folks really are. Then we were off to the city of cardboard.

It was a quiet little community of two or three streets filled with boxes for houses. Some of the better off had a few cinder blocks for walls, no roofs though.

As we pulled in with our rice, beans, and flour, we blew the car horn and people came out knowing they would have something to eat that night. Kids came running up the street for the candy our kids also brought and were handing out.

As they gathered around, we shared a brief message from the Bible in sloppy Spanish. Then we handed out water bottles, food, and gifts. Finishing up we left there with grateful waves of good bye from the children, and we were off to the garbage dump. I had no idea why we were headed to the dump.

Pulling in to an area filled with smoke, we saw piles of garbage burning. "What are we doing here?" I asked. "You just wait and see," our missionary said. He blew his car horn and nothing happened. He blew it again and all of a sudden, out of the smoke, and burning garbage, started to come small figures. Little children covered in ash. It was like a horror movie, only this was real. One by one, they came through the smoke. No shoes and some carrying empty soda bottles. I remember one little girl so black from the smoke you could hardly see her face. Her hair was matted so much you couldn't move it. One of her feet was bleeding from walking in the fire pit looking for bottles. Fortunately one of the adults we had with us on the trip was a nurse, so she cleaned her up and bandaged her foot. What a brave little girl, she didn't even cry.

We had put packages of food and water together to hand out to each one. The children took us past the burning garbage to the area where they lived with their parents. Some had little homes they had made from wood and boards taken from the garbage pile. Others had some cinder block buildings, but again no roofs. The children would

Child running out of garbage dump

go through the garbage and fine soda bottles and trade them in for a cinder block. Five bottles for one block was the going price.

In addition to the food, we gave the girls dolls and the boys Frisbees. I remember one grandma hugging a box of Corn Flakes like it was gold. Looking around I saw our street kids giving these small gifts to the children, and one said to me, "Pastor Nick, we really have it good compared to these people." "Yes," I said. "We get to go back to our air-conditioned bunkhouse, have something cold to drink, and cook some hot dogs over the campfire to eat. They don't leave here. They go back to the burning dump when we leave." I could see a change in all our kids and in the adults too! We left boxes of food and water by the cardboard houses of the folks who were not there at the time. I asked one of the adults, "Aren't you afraid someone will come and take them when we leave?" She said, "Oh no, we are all poor here and would never take what little is given to one of us." Makes you think, doesn't it? In an age when looting is commonplace in our cities where we all have so much.

Onward from there we went to the orphanage. These kids at the orphanage had it a little better. It was government-sponsored so they had nice buildings, furniture, and bathrooms. We brought ice cream and hot dogs with us to celebrate everyone's birthday that was there. Even though our kids and their kids couldn't speak each other's language, they had a great time playing kickball together. We set up my sound system, sang some songs, played some music and had so much fun together we hated to leave, but now our day was done and we headed back to the Mission. Lives had been touched and change on both sides of this giving mission.

Tired and weary from the day we pulled in at dusk. As the headlights lit up the driveway, I couldn't believe what I saw. It was our young man still up in the tree cutting branches with that little hand saw. He had stayed up there all day wanting to get the job done. I told you there was something very special about this kid, and it was beginning to show. We all had dinner together and retired early.

The next morning, before heading home, our missionary took us to a nice Mexican restaurant just on the other side of the border. It was an all-you-can-eat place, which I thought was great for our kids. A real taste of Mexican food.

Lunch was great, and we were really enjoying our time together when the manager came over to me and said, "You have to leave." He had a look of fear on his face. "Oh no, now what" I thought?

"Why, what has happened?" I asked the manager. "Your children have eaten all the food we have, we have no more to put out for our other guests, please leave." This was too funny, but I didn't dare laugh. I know, from past experience, our kids can eat, but never had they eaten a restaurant out of food. It was Mexico, our missionary had brought us there, and our kids had their fill, so I said, "I understand, I'm sorry, we will leave, and thank you so much for the wonderful meal." The manager just gave me a slight nod in the direction of the door.

Heading back home, after saying our goodbyes, you could tell the people we left with three days ago were not the same that were returning. Hearts and minds had changed. God had proven, "When you do it to the least of these, you do it to Me." This would become the first of seven annual trips to Mexico and the Mission House in TX.

Chapter Ten (Triumph)

"But when you do a charitable deed, do not let your left hand know what your right hand is doing, that your charitable deed may be done in secret; and your Father who sees in secret will Himself reward you openly." Matthew 6: 3-4 NKJV

A year and a half passed quickly. Miracles were a daily occurrence for the Center, us, and our supporters. For example; The fellow and his wife who had gotten new furniture for their business and sent us their old furniture, worth about $4,000, received a $31,000.00 check that had been held up from one of their clients and his wife was healed from a five-pound tumor she had that turned out *not* to be cancerous.

God will bless you in many ways when you are striving to follow Him and do His will.

The number of youth we had reached off the streets had grown to 550 and we had outgrown our facilities. The time was approaching to pay $750.00 a month rent or move out. We had made $22,000.00 worth of improvements to the properties so the owner got his money's worth out of us. I was praying daily what to do.

One day in September 1995, as I was starring out the window of our sanctuary building (old renovated bar) I had a vision. Looking across the street at the empty lot that was backed up by one of the worst bars in town, I saw a playground or some type of area with kids playing on it. The terrible bar was now a restaurant where kids were working. Across the street from that the old rundown funeral home was a big worship center with Sunday services. The metal building behind it, where they used to work on their funeral cars, was now a Youth Center where kids were playing. Next to that was a playground filled with playground equipment and kids playing there too. Up the street from the funeral home, but attached to it, was a Christian Shop filled with Christian books and gifts to sell. Kids were working there as well. The vision continued:

Across from that, on the other corner, was a Youth House where kids could stay instead of on the street. Behind that house was a basketball court kids were playing on. Next to that the old Department of Motor Vehicle building was now an Education Building with young people having classes. The vision seemed to last for hours, instead of minutes. Enveloped in this wonderful sight I was rudely snapped back to reality by the words, "Pastor Nick, one of the kids is beating on another!"

The vision stayed with me day after day, week after week, and would not leave me alone. One morning I had a crazy idea. I remembered how God gave Joshua, in the bible, the city of Jericho by just walking around it seven times. I felt I had nothing to lose. Half the people in the town thought I was crazy anyway and the other half could care less what I did, as long as they didn't have to get involved.

"What if I walked around the funeral home building eight times each day until we have to vacate the buildings we are in now?" came the idea. The number eight is the number of new beginnings in the bible. God created the whole world again with eight people after the flood with Noah, his wife, their three sons, and their wives.

If God did answer, I didn't want the walls to fall down, as they did for Joshua when he walked only seven times. Ha!

So, on Monday morning, bright and early at 5:30 A.M., I put on my walking shoes and headed out to the funeral home.

"Okay, God, I'm here. If You want this work to continue, then I ask You to give me this building," that was my prayer.

Police cars would pass by and I would wave. Word had gotten out that the crazy TV Preacher was walking around the funeral home trying to raise the dead or something. Who knows what enters the minds of people when they let their imaginations run wild?

Day after day, week after week, I would walk the building route. Saying the same prayer over and over.

One day in December 1995, I received a call. "Is this Rev. Nick Farone who has the inner city work for the youth?" the voice said. "Yes sir, it is, what can I do for you?" I said. "My two associates and I own the funeral home you have been walking around, and we appreciate the work you are doing," he continued. "Thank you very much, the city surely needs this work," I said. "Yes, we know, and that's why I'm calling. We want to donate that building and property to you for the work of your ministry," he said. There was a long silence after that.

"Hello?" he said on the other end. "Oh, I'm so sorry I thought you said you wanted to give me the funeral home," I said in disbelief. "Yes, that's true, and it comes with the flower shop, work garage, and two-story house on the corner. You can start using them right away, but we will wait a year to sign the actual papers to give us a better tax donation credit after you have fixed them up a bit, if that's okay with you?" he said. "I don't know what to say," I said. "You don't have to say anything, just keep up the good work," he said and hung up the phone.

I was in shock. What a Christmas present this was from God! We met briefly the next day as he handed over the keys to me and said God Bless you. God didn't give me one building, He gave me three, plus half a city block to do with what I saw in the vision.

I went directly from his office to the funeral home. I entered the side door under the carport they had and went into the main building. In the dark, on the bare concrete floor, I knelt down and thanked God for this great miracle. I could not wait to tell the folks on Sunday that God had blessed us with our own, permanent home to worship, minister, and grow. My walking days were over, for the time being.

Chapter Eleven (Triumph)

"No weapon formed against you shall prosper, And every tongue which rises against you in judgment You shall condemn, This is the heritage of the servants of the Lord. And their righteousness is from Me, says the Lord." Isaiah 54:17 NKJV

The first thing we did was to build three crosses in the play area outside the future Youth Center building. I placed them so that when you stood at the foot of the cross of Christ you could look straight ahead and see the old buildings where it all started in the rundown bar.

Little by little, we started to move things over to our new facilities. First on the agenda was to get the old tin building converted into a big Youth Center to continue getting kids off the streets. God was bringing in people from outside the city, as well as inside the city, to accomplish His purpose for His children. One friend said, "Ask me to do anything but paint." Guess what we needed him to do? He graciously consented and did a great job. Old broken windows were fixed. Electrical wiring repaired. New ceilings were installed. Some of the Youth we were working with helped us paint the outside. I think they got more paint on themselves than the building. You must always be encouraging when you know someone is doing their best. One youth helped and did a

Three crosses

wonderful job painting everything he saw. There he was, covered in paint from head to toe, admiring his work. I walked up to congratulate him and said, "You did a great job, just one thing, next time you don't have to paint the glass on the windows." I spent the next day with scrapper in hand, undoing some of this proud young man's hard work.

It was all coming together. Some churches even started to get involved. One gave us some used table games for the Center. Another gave us some used chairs. Finally, the city had a Youth Center that all kids could come to and they didn't have to be a part of a particular denomination. Things were going great, too great, for some in that city.

Chapter Twelve (Trial)

Saying, Do not touch My anointed ones…"
1 Chronicles 16:22 NKJV

I'm an Ordained Bishop with the Church of God, and I'm privileged to be so. I wasn't always a part of their particular denomination in my twenty-nine years of ministry. Making New Beginnings an Interdenominational work, meaning for all kids, got some upset in the city.

One church, in particular, took great offense. They had disagreements with their former pastor and forced him out of the city. I had been greatly received at this particular church for many years, and the pastor and I were great friends. One day I was asked to speak about their pastor's decision to leave. Entering the pulpit the people were anxious to hear my thoughts, until they heard what they were.

"Your pastors love you and I am sure if you ask them to stay they would," I said. There was dead silence and then shouts of disagreements. "Furthermore, God has called me to do a work here in the city for the Youth, and I would very much like you to be part of it, but we will do it with or without your help," I said. That was like throwing down the gauntlet.

Soon after that, I got a call from my state office asking me to come in. I thought it was to give me recognition for all the wonderful work we had been doing with the youth and for our newly donated facilities. WRONG!

Sitting in the outer office waiting for my appointed time I saw all the awards for various works displayed on the walls. I felt maybe they wanted to post something for us to honor the work we were doing with the kids. "So-and-so will see you now," the secretary said coldly.

Upon entering his office, he rose from behind his large desk, reached across it, and gave me a handshake. "Sit down, Rev. Farone," he said. I felt a chill in that handshake and in the room. I slowly lowered myself into the big leather chair in front of his desk. It was so big it made me feel small, like a kid myself. I'm sure now that was its particular function.

"Rev. Farone, I have had reports that you have established an inner city 'Interdenominational' work, is that right?" he said. "Yes sir, it's been there almost two years now and doing quite well," I said. "Well, we have had some complaints filed against you from one of the churches you used to minister at in the city, which has recently lost their pastor," he said. "Complaints?" I was caught off guard. "Yes, I won't go into detail, but I want to get right to the point. We appreciate the work you are doing with the youth and we want you to continue, but we want you to make the work a denominational work, *our denomination*, that you are a part of," he said. "Well, I'd like to do that, sir, but I have kids coming from all denominations and I just want them to focus on Jesus being their Lord and Savior to change their lives. I still preach and teach the full Gospel message our denomination believes and I will continue, but if I make it solely one denomination I won't be able to reach all the kids we are reaching now," I said and felt he would understand.

"To simplify things, let me say this," he said. "You are an Evangelist with our denomination and based out of California, is that correct?" "Yes sir," I said. "Well, in our national rules you are free to minister in any state as long as the Director of the State agrees and I, being the Director, am telling you unless you make your work part of our denomination, with its name included in your promotions, I will not agree to have you here working in our state."

It was another of those pause moments; I didn't know what to say or do. Shaking my head and his hand, I slowly left the chamber of horrors and went home.

The folks in the church who reported me knew I would choose God and His direction over a denomination. They just didn't want me part of theirs any more. After I had seen what they did to their former pastors, I felt I had no choice but to leave the organization I loved and had many friends in. This was a trial I didn't see coming.

Heading home to tell Sandy, I had a lot of time to think about things. The choice was obvious. Look at all God had done. Many times, when we are faced with circumstances that turn our lives upside down, we forget all that God has done in the past. Our values will be tested constantly. As for me and my house, we will serve the Lord.

Arriving home, I told Sandy and she was 100 percent behind my decision. The church got what they wanted. On that following Monday, I wrote my letter of resignation to the state office and the national headquarters.

I have always ministered in many denominational venues, so my ministry didn't stop outside the city. Pastor friends, whose churches I had ministered in for years, just ignored the Louisiana verdict and let me still come and share God's Word and message. My messages were actually growing and being used by God even more. He was showing me my choice was correct.

About two months later, I received a letter from the national office stating that they were sorry to see me go and that I had been a wonderful blessing to the organization. They also said to let them know when I wanted to come back and there would be no problem. The amazing thing was, on the same day I received their letter, I received another letter inviting me to be ordained with a similar organization. They had the same name and same doctrine, but they didn't mind I was establishing an interdenominational work. This was another witness from God I had made His choice, the right choice.

Chapter Thirteen (Triumph)

"Trust in the Lord, and do good; Dwell in the Land, and feed on His faithfulness." Psalm 37: 3 NKJV

Back at the ranch, Youth Center to be accurate, my daily praying two hours was being honored by God. I know some people will say it makes no difference how long you pray. I have to tell you, everything we needed was being sent in just through those prayers.

We began restoring and using the two-story white house. It needed major work and an air conditioning unit. We also needed some steel bar doors now on the Youth Center to keep all the things we had received for the youth from being stolen in that neighborhood.

The total amount I needed was $10,000.00. I never told our specific financial needs in the services I would do out of town. This was a big one, and I knew I would have to stay on the road doing services for a long time to raise that amount of money.

Our friends in California were great supporters of our ministry by having us for services at their church. They were the first church God had me schedule seeking this need. Their church attendance that morning was about forty people, and the service was blessed with God's presence.

After service, I was packing up my sound equipment and the pastor came up to me. He said, "Nick, we are counting the offering, but this

Old youth center building front

House with tree in front

check was made out directly to you for your ministry so I'll just give it to you."

I took the check, and it was for $1,000.00. That was a tremendous offering from one person. I was elated.

About five minutes after putting the check in my pocket, a lady came up to me and said, "Excuse me, Pastor Nick, I'm the one who gave you the check for $1,000.00 and I'd like it back." To avoid my shock and disappointment, I said, "Excuse me one minute please, I'll be right back." I walked over to the corner and said under my breath to God, "God, what are You doing, I don't understand, what did I do?"

Walking back over to the lady I handed her the check, as gracefully as possible. I had a hard time letting go of my end of the check, but I found the strength. Taking the check out of my hand she said, "As I was leaving God spoke to me and said not to give you the check for $1,000.00. He said you needed $10,000.00." Then she corrected the check to $10,000.00, handed it to me, and walked away. I stood there stunned for a minute or two watching her leave the church. I will never forget her.

After my service that evening, I headed back to Louisiana and ordered the things we needed. Now the Youth Center was secure and the House was ready for caretakers and kids.

Chapter Fourteen (Trial)

"For God so loved the world that He gave His only begotten Son, that whoever believes in Him should not perish, but have everlasting life." John 3:16 NKJV

Remember our young man who barely looked up the first few weeks during services at the original center? Well, by now he came every day to work with me, when he wasn't at his small job. We were becoming friends, and he was speaking up now more and more. My messages from God's word were reaching him.

One day I saw him with his sheet rock knife cutting off the dirty words from his arm. I walked up to him and said, "What are you doing?" He said, "Mr. Nick," he never called me Pastor and that was okay with me. "I don't want God to be ashamed of me, so I'm cutting these off," he said. I said, "God looks at your heart, not at the outside, He knows you and He loves you just the way you are." I took the sheet rock knife from him, and I still have it today. He got my message and never got another one. He and some of the other boys were growing, and a wonderful event came up for us "Men" to attend.

In July an organization called, "Promise Keepers" was having a big night in New Orleans at the Stadium. We got a van full of our boys and went. What a great weekend of music and speakers it turned out to be.

You could feel the presence of the Lord all around you. Our boys had a great time.

On the long ride home, that evening, we were all talking about the event. There is a twenty-two mile long bridge that goes over the bayou on the drive home. We decided to share what each one of us thought of the events to pass the time. On this trip home something happened that was strange. As we rode along listening to the thumping of the tires, in the quiet time, our once gang leader young man had his head resting against the window and all he kept saying was, "God has changed me, God has changed me, God has changed me." All the way home that was all he said, "God has changed me."

The next morning at Sunday service you could feel the electricity in the air. The boys were all still excited, from the night before. I asked them to share what they liked the most about the event. Some got up and said they enjoyed the music. Some got up and said they enjoyed a particular speaker. Then our young leader in training stood up. He spoke clearly and boldly for the first time.

"I want to say God has changed me," he said with a loud voice. "I am going to be that Youth Leader Pastor Nick says I can be," then he sat down. That was the first time he ever called me "Pastor." I began to tear up so we started to sing some praise and worship songs. He began to sing, and he had a beautiful voice. "You have a beautiful voice, you should sing more," Sandy said to him, and he smiled from ear to ear.

After service, we had two young men come down and kneel at the altar. They were gang members that came to service for the first time and heard our new Youth Leader's testimony that morning.

"Pastor Nick, we want you to make us Youth Leaders too," they said. "I can't, but if you will give your life to Jesus, He will," I said. Right there they said the sinner's prayer with me and gave their lives over to Jesus. They thanked Him for dying for their sins, and it was our new Youth Leader's testimony that brought them to the foot of the cross.

That evening on **July 28, 1996,** I got a call at our home. "Pastor Nick," the voice on the other end said, "Can I stay at the Youth House?

I really want to be that Youth Leader for you and be right there at the Center." He was so excited he could hardly contain himself. "That would be fantastic and I'm all for it, but we must always honor our parents so you will have to okay it with your mother," I said. "I will right away," he said and hung up the phone.

A few minutes later he called back. "Hello?" I said. There was a long pause on the other end of the phone. "Hello?" I said again. "Pastor Nick, I told my mom what I wanted to do and she said no. She also said I am never to come back to New Beginnings," he said and hung up the phone.

I didn't know what to do. Jesus had changed his life. He had so much to give and was excited about his life for the first time in the year and a half I knew him. I felt I would sleep on it and deal with it in the morning.

About half an hour later I got a call from the Sheriff's Department. "Pastor Nick, am I old enough to make my own decisions," it was our Youth Leader again. "Why are you calling me from the Sheriff's Office?" I asked. "Here's the Sheriff," he said and put him on the phone. "Nick, this young man here wants to move into your Youth House and he says his mother won't let him. He asked me if he was old enough to make his own decision and being eighteen years old, I told him he was. What do you want me to do?" he said. The Sheriff and I were friends, so I asked him, "What do you think I should do?" "Nick, I know this family, and this is his opportunity to break from the bad influence they all have and get a fresh start. If it were me, I'd tell him yes. As a matter of fact, I'll go there right now and help him move his things over there, if you want?" he said.

Our young man had truly changed. Jesus had turned his life around. He was, at that moment, as far as I was concerned, God's new Youth Leader at the Center. "Go ahead and help him, I agree he needs a new home," I said.

That very night he moved into his own room at the Youth House, and there was a big celebration. Our caretakers bought some ice cream and cake to celebrate. What a change we had seen in this young man.

Everyone who knew him could see there was a new person from the one they all feared. From stabbing tires, carving dirty words into his arm, being ready to fight at the drop of a hat, into someone who now only wanted to live and serve Jesus, his Lord and Savior. I couldn't wait to see what God would do with His new Youth Leader. New Beginnings was changing lives; he was the proof.

It was 7:00 A.M. Monday morning, a day I will remember the rest of my life. I got a call from the Youth House. "Nick, come quick, I can't wake him up and he's cold," our caretaker said. I was there by 7:04 A.M.

Running upstairs to his first room of his own, I saw him lying on his bed. He wasn't breathing. When I went to do CPR on him, his body was already cold and stiff. "Call 911," I screamed. Within minutes, the Fire Dept. was there, trying to revive him, but they knew, as I did, it was too late. The Coroner arrived soon after them and pronounced him dead. He said he believed he passed sometime during the night.

Keeping my composure as long as I could, I left the house and ran to the three crosses we had placed in our playground. Wrapping my arms around the one in the middle, that represented Jesus, I fell to my knees yelling, "Why?" "Why?" Why?" I don't know how long I was there. Overcome with anger I stood to my feet, turned away from the cross, and screamed, "Devil, you may have killed this one, but you didn't get him. He's with his Lord now, and I promise you this. From this day forward I am going to get ten more to honor him, in the name of Jesus I vow."

Somehow, my composure returned and I dealt with the rest of the day.

The Coroner found that he had a grand mall seizure. He apparently had seizures all his life. He was taking medication to control them. What was amazing to me was, in all the time that we spent together, I never once saw him have a seizure or take any medications. I believe it was the calm of God's Holy Spirit that kept him when we were together. That night when he went to the Youth House, to have a new home, the emotional stress from dealing with his mother and the joy of being free was too much for him. That was the explanation I was given.

I had to do something to honor what God had done in this young man's life. I decided to have a community service and dedicate the Youth House to him as our first Youth Leader. I would do a service in August and invite his mother, so she could be proud of her son's legacy.

I had made several attempts to contact his mom, but she was never at home when I went by. Then one day, a week before the planned dedication service, I saw her walking downtown. I stopped to tell her of the wonderful tribute we were giving her son and was shocked at her response. "You stay the hell away from me and my family," she screamed in my face and walked away. Then I heard another voice that was calm and affirming. "That's why I took him home, Nick," Jesus said.

Our new Youth Leader did move to a new home. One far greater than the one he expected. A home His Lord had already prepared for him.

In August we held an outdoor ceremony dedicating the Youth House to him.

Chapter Fifteen (Triumph)

"Now I say this, that each of you says, "I am of Paul," or "I am of Apollos," or "I am Cephas," or "I am of Christ." 1 Corinthians 1:12 NKJV

To tell you the truth, leaving one denomination for another really didn't affect me or our work. The important thing in life is to have Jesus Christ as your Savior. It so angered the church organization I had been with that they kept trying us in various ways. The more they tried, the more God would bless us. Let me tell you, when God starts to bless you it is going to upset some people. Don't be surprised if it's some of the people you thought you knew.

Trials are part of life, you can't avoid them. But as a child of God, you can walk through them and see miracles. Miracles you can share with others to bring encouragement. Some will hear and accept what you are doing. Some will hear and deny. Some won't even want to hear about it. That's okay! We are not made to convince, we are made to share and let God's Holy Spirit do the convincing.

Christmas 1996 was upon us and the time for signing of the donation papers was at hand. It would be one of the largest donations in the city's history. We had established a permanent Youth Center and were now meeting in the old refurbished funeral home for services on Sunday.

Church pews were donated to us all the way from a church in Mississippi. We had fixed the drop ceilings in the main building that had all collapsed from all the years the building just sat there. My sound system fit perfectly in the sanctuary area, as did the kneelers my friend George made from the old pool table. We had all we needed, but it was still a struggle each week to pay new light bills, water bills, and heating bills. When most people give they don't think of the basics you need money for, they just want to see something big happening. God didn't let them down. That's exactly what people saw, big things happening every week.

Chapter Sixteen (Trial)

"...When the enemy comes in like a flood, The Spirit of the Lord will lift up a standard against him." Isaiah 59:19 NKJV

As soon as we started using the Youth Center, Youth House, and Main Building for church services on Sundays, I had a problem.

On Friday and Saturday nights, the terrible bar across the street, which had been parking their patrons' cars in our parking lot, wanted to keep doing it. This could no longer be the case. I had kids there now at their Youth Center, and I wanted that bad influence across the street, where it belonged.

The very first Sunday, after service was over, I was approached by someone from the bar. "Excuse me, I run the bar across the street," he said. "We have been using this parking lot for years. I want to give you a weekly offering to help your church if you will let us keep parking our cars here on Friday and Saturday nights."

"Well, I'm sorry, but this is God's property now and your parking days here are over," I said. Getting as close to my face as he could, where I could tell what gum he was chewing to cover up his liquor breath, he said, "You don't understand who you are dealing with. You are going to get hurt!"

Okay, now even though I am a born again child of God and preacher in God's service, I am still a New York Sicilian/Italian. Without moving my face from his glare, I said, "You don't know who you are dealing with. I'm from New York and if you don't move your cars, I will have them towed."

He moved away from my face and walked back across the street.

Early that following Monday morning, Sandy and some ladies in our congregation went across the street and prayed God would shut down this bar that was such a bad influence on His children. Watch out when real women of prayer get together!

Three months later the man was arrested for selling liquor to a minor, put in jail, and the bar was closed.

We soon learned there is a law on the books that if a bar is in the vicinity of a church, before the church was there, it was allowed to stay. But now that it was closed, it could never reopen again as a bar. The law says you cannot open a bar within 500 feet of a church. God works in mysterious ways His wonders to perform.

Chapter Seventeen (Triumph)

"...For everyone to whom much is given, from him much will be required; and to whom much has been committed, of him they will ask the more." Luke 12:48 NKJV

Two months later, we received another call from someone we didn't know.

"Is this Rev. Nick Farone who has the Youth Ministry on Pine Street?" the man said. "Yes it is, how can I help you?" I said. "You don't know me, but I own the building and property across the street from your ministry. There used to be a bar there. Since it closed down I would like to donate that building and property to your ministry," he said.

"That would be great!" I said. "Oh, and the property also includes part of the corner lot as well. You might want to do something with that for the kids," he said. "I'll get the papers drawn up and be in touch," he said and ended his conversation.

God was giving me the bar I saw as a restaurant in my vision and part of the corner lot I saw as a play area. This was truly amazing.

In March 1997, we were given two more parts of the vision I had in September 1995.

We began work immediately, painting the outside all white, covering up the devil's artwork on the bar.

Three months later I received another phone call from Mobile, AL.

"Is this Rev. Nick Farone?" a women's voice on the other end said. "Yes ma'am," I said. "You don't know me. I live in Mobile, AL, and I own the corner lot across from your Center, I hear you have for Youth," she said. "Yes, that's right, what can I do for you?" I said.

"I want to donate that to you to use for something for the Youth. I'll have the papers drawn up and send them to you," she said. "Thank you so much, I don't know what to say," I said. "No need to say anything, just keep up the good work," she said and hung up.

On **July 29, 1997**, we now owned the old bar and the complete corner lot.

It was a year to the day our first Youth Leader died, and I had made my vow to get ten more for Jesus.

Chapter Eighteen (Triumph)

"For even in Thessalonica you sent aid once and again for my necessities. Not that I seek the gift, but seek the fruit that abounds to your account. Indeed I have all and abound. I am full, having received from Epaphroditus the things sent from you, a sweet-smelling aroma, an acceptable sacrifice, well pleasing to God." Philippians 4: 16-18 NKJV

God was again proving Himself faithful to His word and promises. Our Prayer Partners and churches we ministered in across the country were building the center by their giving. Even a couple of churches, in the city of churches, were beginning to support us now. The minister at the Methodist church and I became friends. His congregation started to see what we were doing and wanted to help, so they came up with a plan. They asked what I needed. It was the basketball court I saw in my vision to get the kids coming more often to the Center. The boys could only play so much pool or ping pong, but they would play basketball around the clock if you would let them. The plan they came up with was to do a *"Musical Salute to America"* for the Fourth of July holiday at their church. It would be a benefit for New Beginnings and all the proceeds would go towards putting in a basketball court. I would be one of the participants. God was softening some hearts for us in the city.

The benefit program went great, and we raised $2,300.00, which was enough for the concrete and materials. Our wonderful friends at the church in Covington, LA, came to the Center and brought some other friends to do all the physical labor. These were exciting times in the ministry.

Basketball Court

Chapter Nineteen (Trial)

"Not everyone who says, Lord, Lord, shall enter the kingdom of heaven, but he who does the will of My Father in heaven." Matthew 7:21 NKJV

He came forward and gave his heart to the Lord at my service in California. That means he repented of his sins and turned his life over to Jesus, trusting Him to take over and guide him. Jesus paid the price for his sins and now would give him a new life.

He was six foot, three inches tall, and 220 pounds. He had been in jail and lived a life of drugs, drinking, and hard living. His pastor believed he had changed in his spirit and made a commitment to change his life as well. The best way to do that was to get away from old friends and make new ones. New friends who lived a lifestyle opposite from the one he had been living.

His pastor raised the money and sent him to us. When he arrived, we had just gone through a big disappointment from people who professed one thing but lived another and were leery of accepting another from out of town. Yet, how can you refuse trying to help someone better their life, especially if they are trying to follow Jesus? After all, Jesus came to seek and save the lost, right? That's what New Beginnings is all about.

When he arrived we gave him a place to live, paid his utilities, and even raised a salary of $200.00 a week for his personal needs. Sometimes that was more income than Sandy, Nicky, and I received for ourselves as a family of three to live on. We had a Board Member give him his car to use so he would have his own personal transportation. You couldn't miss the car, it was painted bright green. The kids fell in love with him. He was so big they literally looked up to him as their protector. He was a hard worker and helped me renovate the future restaurant building. When gang members would pass by the Youth Center, they would see this towering figure looming in the front door and think twice about causing any trouble.

For about a year things were going great with his new life. There was one thing that puzzled me, though. He never seemed to have any money. I'd pay him on Friday and by Tuesday he'd be broke. He literally had no expenses. All he really needed money for was food and personal needs. Most of the time he would eat with us or at the special outings we would take the kids on, yet he was always broke. What you do with your money is your business, I didn't pry. If you are doing something wrong, you will be found out, especially if you are around kids. Kids will rat you out, no doubt about it!

"Pastor Nick, there was a girl in the Youth House," came the first report. When I asked our "professing Christian" about it, he said no, there wasn't, the kids were lying. The next report came from an adult that supported our ministry.

"Pastor Nick, I think I saw that green car parked at one of the casinos two hours away in another city," they said. Now, that bright green car is hard to mistake, so I asked him about this report. No, it wasn't him, he didn't even know where the casino was, he said.

Time passed, and it came time for one of our Missions trips to Mexico and our new helper went with us. We all noticed he was drinking a lot of water. We would have stop two or three times the normal potty breaks on the way down and back. Each time we stopped, he would guzzle a gallon of water. I was concerned so when we got back,

I set up an appointment with our family doctor to take a look and see what was up. He was reluctant, but went for his physical. We had a wonderful family doctor. He was one of the true blessings God gave us while we were facing a city that resented what we were doing for the unwanted children. His report would open the floodgates of truth that had to be exposed.

"Nick, I hate to tell you this, but your friend has a venereal disease. It's pretty bad, so I've started him on treatments," Doc said. I went to see him right away and he now confessed all that was said about him, was true. The reason he was always broke on Tuesday was that he would take his paycheck on Monday and go to the casinos. Not just one of them, all of them. He had also met a wounded vet, just outside the city, who was supplying him with marijuana he would grow right at his home. Finally, he did occasionally have a woman at the Youth House when he thought it was late and everyone else was asleep.

So, we said bye-bye to our Brother. "Boy can I pick em," I said to myself. There is no easy life and none of us is perfect, but you must be what you profess to be, if you are going to reach children for God. They will see right through you in no time. God will also expose it if you are professing to be His servant and doing His work, but hiding an alternate lifestyle. Back to being short-handed, again....

Chapter Twenty (Triumph)

"So Jesus said to them, "Because of your unbelief; for assuredly, I say to you, if you have faith as a mustard seed, you will say to this mountain, Move from here to there, and it will move; and nothing will be impossible for you." Matthew 17:20 NKJV

By now my faith to trust God for everything was growing, and I started to believe even more for the impossible.

We had five buildings to restore, playgrounds, parking lots, and kids coming from everywhere. Poor "Job" (our van) was limping along with his new motor the best he could. I was happy just to have him to do all the things we were doing with the kids.

Driving along one of the main streets in another city close to us one day, I passed a Ford dealership. That voice, His voice, always catches me off guard. "I want you to ask them if they have a new, white, fifteen-passenger van, with seatbelts all around, and give them 'Job' as a trade in." Ha! Ha! Ha! Ha! I needed a good laugh that day.

Then God brought ***Matthew 17:20*** to my mind, and I turned around in faith.

"So Jesus said to them, "Because of your unbelief, for assuredly, I say to you, if you have faith as a mustard seed, you will

say to this mountain, move from here to there and it will move; and nothing will be impossible for you."

Pulling up in front of the dealership one of the sales people came running out. "Can I help you," he said. "Yes, I want to know if you have a new, white, fifteen-passenger van, with seatbelts all around for sale?" I said. He said, "Please, do me a favor would you park your van around back so we can keep this spot clear?" I knew what he was saying. "Job" didn't look the best for his age and was sort of an eyesore, if you know what I mean.

"Okay, sure, no problem," I said.

Walking inside to the man's office and sitting down, he was very polite. "I'll just be a minute, I have to check our inventory," he said. "Would you like some coffee, soda, or water while you wait?" "No, I'm fine, thank you," I said.

About ten or fifteen minutes passed and the salesman returned. "Yes, we have just one and it only has twenty-five miles on it, right off the truck," he sounded hopeful. "Great!" I said. "I'll take it." Boy my faith was flying high that day. "Okay, I'll do a credit check, and do you have a trade in you'd like to use?" he said. "Yes, you just had me move him around back, his name is 'Job,'" I said.

The salesman's elation disappeared, but he went to do the credit check anyway.

It seemed like a lifetime passed, but it was only thirty minutes and he returned. "Okay we will give you $600 for 'Job,' we have a dealer's discount right now for $2,500.00, and you can have so much percentage financing, because your credit is A plus, what do you say?" he said. I said, "Show me the Money!" No, only kidding, I said, "Bring me the papers we have a deal."

That morning I drove into that dealership with 'Job', and that evening I drove home, from the dealership, in "Faith." That's what we named our new 1997, fifteen-passenger, white van, with seatbelts all around. The payments were $425.00 a month and God supplied that for six years faithfully. We even paid the van off early. Triumph!

Me and our faithful red van "Job"

Our new 1997 White Ford van

Chapter Twenty-One (Triumph)

"This is the refreshing." Isaiah 28:12 NKJV

Time was passing quickly, and I was starting to feel the weight of all that was on my shoulders.

Now we had a future restaurant, an active Youth Center, an active Youth House, an active Christian Shop, an active Main Building for services, and office space for me. Yet, we only had eight adults holding this all together. I spent a lot of my time on the road sharing and raising funds to keep it all going. I was worn out, and God knew it.

I was in Florida doing services at a church I had never been to before, with a pastor I had never met. My friend Charles, who got the invite for me, was now their Associate Pastor. Service went wonderful, and we had many come to the altar to give their hearts to the Lord. Lives were changed. The pastor said to me, "Nick, I'd like to invite you to come with us this week to a Promise Keepers meeting just for pastors, as my treat. I'll pay all the expenses for you, what do you say?" I was so thankful that he would do this for me, what else could I say, but "Yes."

I called Sandy, who was holding down the fort at the Center, and told her of this generous offer. She said, "That's wonderful, don't worry about back here, just go and enjoy yourself."

The following day we headed out to the Georgia Dome in Atlanta, GA. It would be one of those life-changing experiences for me. Forty thousand pastors were there from all over the country. You could see on their faces the burdens and stress each man carried. Some were about to give up and relinquish their call from all the trials they had faced trying to serve people in ministry. Ministry had finally taken its toll. Even though we didn't know each other, there was a kindred spirit.

God began to speak to my heart in a special way. It was the third song of the night. It started with a single note. Then a snare drum was added, followed by a simple melody, played on the piano. To the right of the stage was a small group of men who stepped forward and began to sing softly, "*Let the Cross be our glory and the Lord be our song.*" The spirit in the men began to change. A giant jumbo screen was lowered with the words and music on it, and some of us began to sing along with the chorus. By the third verse, the whole arena began to vibrate with God's presence. Men were singing together, raising their hands in praise, unashamed to give honor and glory to the One we all served. I knew I just had to share this moment with Sandy wishing she were there with me. I pulled out my cell phone and called her. She picked up on the first ring and I said, "Listen!" then I held the phone out so she could hear what I was hearing. For about three minutes we shared it together. "Isn't this amazing?" I said. "Yes that's awesome," Sandy said, and we lost connection. "Thank you, God," I said. Vendors left their stands around the arena to see what was going on. As soon as they entered the arena, they were stopped in their tracks by a power only described as majestic. The song ended on a quiet note, and no one moved. You could have heard a pin drop. The silence would be broken by one man in the crowd weeping. Then another and another. Pastors who had never met each other before were hugging as they cried out their pain. Not knowing what pain the other was carrying, only knowing that at that moment they were all being healed. Some were being healed in their bodies, some in their minds, and all forty thousand in their spirits. At that moment we all knew that no matter what we would face in the days ahead, we would make it through because Jesus Himself would be at each and every one of our sides. It was an event I will never forget.

I turned to tell my friend standing next to me what I had just done with my cell phone with Sandy and he said, "That's impossible. This is an all metal building and you can't get cell reception in here." Then he tried, but was unable to get any reception, just as he said. Others around me tried as well, but none were successful. Only I received this blessing, and my words to Sandy became prophetic: "Isn't this amazing." I didn't know how much until that moment. That was the beginning of the miracles God had planned for me at this event.

Each speaker was tremendous, and all the messages were prepared to encourage those forty-thousand servants of our Lord. As I stood there listening to one of the speakers, God was speaking to the pastor who I had just met and brought me on this trip. He came over to where I was standing and said, "God has told me to give you a gift." "What, excuse me, what did you say?" I said. "God has told me to give you my watch," he said. This was strange. I hadn't even noticed he was wearing a watch. "It's solid gold with a couple of diamonds. I got it in Alaska, and it's worth about $500.00," he said.

I thought to myself, "God, I don't want to take the man's watch. I'll probably sell it and use the money to buy something for the Center." I had no sooner finished my silent conversation with God when the pastor said, "Now, you can sell it if you want to, but God is telling me to tell you He is going to pour out His blessings on you and the Center and you will never have to sell your watch. It is yours to remind you of His faithfulness," he said.

Taking off his watch and giving it to me, he added, "Now, you may have to have it sized to fit your wrist." I said, "If God is giving me your watch, it will fit." I put it on my wrist, and it fit perfectly. What else could I say but, "Thank You!" The speaker finished, and we both went back to our seats.

In the years ahead God would truly use this watch as a testimony to His promise to me that day to bless the ministry and my life personally.

Gold Watch

Chapter Twenty-Two (Triumph)

"Now to Him who is able to do exceedingly abundantly above all that we ask or think, according to the power that works in us." Ephesians 3:20 NKJV

I felt so refreshed returning to the Center and was able to begin work again on this journey God had laid out for us. What about our son who was now twelve years old, how was God taking care of him, you may ask.

There came into our lives one seemingly ordinary person who God would use to do the extraordinary for our son, Dominick Jr.

This choice servant of God hasn't written any books. He didn't have a TV ministry. He wasn't even in the ministry as a minister. God just had him waiting for us, though neither of us knew it. We met him back in 1992 at a Christian Camp for children, only ten miles from our home in Louisiana. We had parked our travel trailer there overnight as we did services one Sunday morning. He was a lanky ol' fella, with cowboy boots and a Texan hat. He had an easy goin' way about him and made his living selling cattle and farming. Some locals said, "He sure knew how to make money." But the love of his life was the Lord. The next was his wife. He'd kick up his heels and sing the hymns with the best of them.

In 1974 he donated 140 acres to build a camp to reach children for Jesus. He helped convert an old barn into a chapel where folks met on

Saturday nights for food and fellowship. Folks of all denominations who just wanted to worship their Lord together. In 1979 they built their first dorm to house children during a one-week summer camp. Together they also built an open-air gym in 1984. In 1994 they built a screened-in amphitheater.

By 2002 they had a chapel, open-air gym, dining hall, archery range, sixty-four bed dormitory, five weeks of summer camp for children, amphitheater, swimming pool, ropes course, and all to the glory of God. This fella was someone who knew his Lord, believed His word, and refused to give up. "Nick, just keep goin'," he'd say to me many times when things got rough. "Don't be bothered by those who don't see what you see or disagree with your ways," he'd say. "That's how the Lord built this place." His words and example kept me going many times during my trials.

Ever since Dominick Jr. was old enough to attend Summer Camp, this modern day saint would give him a full scholarship to attend each year. Eventually Dominick Jr. became one of the camp counselors. Then one year he met the most amazing, beautiful girl that took his breath and her heart away. Her name is Jacqui. It was love at first sight

for both of them. God gave me the privilege of officiating at their wedding on June 2, 2007.

A friend of ours in Oregon gave me these words of encouragement as he watched our ministry growing. "Nick, never forget when God calls a man into His ministry, He calls the whole family to trust Him as well. He will provide for you *and* your family." Those words have proven true time and again. Thank you, my friend.

Sandy home-schooled Dominick Jr. for the first few years as we traveled on the road, in the back seat of our car and in campgrounds. When God provided a home for us, He also provided Christian Schools for Dominick Jr. to attend, all the way through ORU College in Tulsa, OK.

The year of their eighth anniversary, there's that number eight again, **Dominick Jr. III** would make his arrival on July 7, 2015. Hee! Hee! God is amazing!

So, whatever it is God has placed on your heart to do, in the words of my ol' friend, "Just keep going."

He won't let you down.

Chapter Twenty-Three (Triumph)

"Assuredly, I say to you, unless you are converted and become as little children, you will by no means enter the kingdom of heaven." Matthew 18:3 NKJV

"Did you hear about James?" Sandy said.

At eight years old, he was one of the little ones coming to the center. We noticed he had a "Mr. Magoo" type squint. So one day, when I saw him with his face buried in a book using his nose as a pointer, I walked over and said, "Can't you see good?" His reply was always cheerful, "Yes, I see good!" then he just shrugged it off and went to play.

The next week I shared his story at a Women's meeting I was invited to speak at in Leland, MS, and one of the ladies came up and gave me a check to buy our little James some glasses. God is so good.

The following day I had his eyes tested by a local optometrist and found out that he could not see more than two feet in front of him. It took a while for this little guy to remember to wear his glasses, but whenever he would show up at the Center without them, one of us would remind him and he'd be off to get them and back in no time, enjoying his whole new world of sight. He improved at everything, even his disposition, if that was possible, for he already had a natural sweet spirit. Everything was great with him except that routine statement he'd make when you first saw him. "Can I have fifty cents?"

The first couple of times I couldn't resist that innocent little face and gave him fifty cents.

One day I said to him, "Hey, come here. Why should I give you fifty cents?" He said, "I don't know." Then I said, "If I give you fifty cents I'll have to give fifty cents to everyone here to be fair. We all share everything here, do you understand?" He shook his head and ran over to the bleeping Nintendo game. As he ran, God gave me an idea and I called out to him, "Yo, little James, wait a minute, would you like to earn fifty cents?" He shot back over to me. "What can I do?" he said. "Do you see those papers and cups lying on the floor over there in the corner?" I said, pointing to the trash. "If you will pick them up for me I'll give you fifty cents."

Faster than a speeding bullet, more powerful than a locomotive, and able to leap tall chairs in a single bound, he was gone and so was the trash.

The next day, when he came running in, I expected to hear those famous words, "Can I have fifty cents?" But I was taken back. "Pastor Nick, what can I do for you today for fifty cents?" he said. I said, "Well, there's some stuff outside we need to have picked up." In the blink of an eye he was gone and so was the stuff. Word spread like a wild fire. Now I had a workforce. "Pastor Nick, Pastor Nick, Pastor Nick, what can I do for fifty cents?" God had created a team of young people cleaning up their Center and taking pride in how it looked. Weeds pulled, grass mowed, dirt swept, buildings painted (minus windows), they were becoming fishers for fish and not beggars. They were also starting to have self worth and even smile more. God had given me an idea, through this little boy, that would touch those attending the Center for years to come. Back to my story and Sandy's question....

I said to Sandy, "What happened to our little 'Glasses James'?"

"Do you remember on Friday, when he came in to give me my daily hug, I asked him to pray for you about the convention you are going to speak at this week?" Sandy said. "Sure," I said. "Well, the person watching the center for us said she found him kneeling in the middle of the parking lot, last night, and he wasn't moving, with his face in his hands." Sandy continued. "She said she got nervous and ran over to him. "Are you all right" she said? "Yes," he said, "I'm okay." So she asked him, "Well, then why are you in the middle of the parking lot with your face in your hands?" He looked up at her and said so matter-of-factly, "I'm praying for Pastor Nick." And there I was wiping my eyes as Sandy and I entered the plane to take our seats.

I'm so thankful to God for what He is doing in the lives of these little ones most people have given up on but He never will.

If only we adults would learn from their example. As adults, we tend to stray from the simple things God tells us to do, unless times get hard. Prayer is usually the first thing to go. If we would spend more time on our knees sharing with God, we would see His miracles happen more in our own lives. After all, we are His children.

Chapter Twenty-Four (Trial)

Jesus said to him, "He who is bathed needs only to wash his feet, but is completely clean; and you are clean, but not all of you." John 13:10 NKJV

Let's face it, life is full of trials and we must deal with them, put them in the past, and focus on the positives. I want my readers to know that when you come upon a trial God wants you to go through, He may be exposing something only He sees. Much like going to a doctor who sees something in an x-ray that is causing you harm, but not visible to the naked eye. Once it is dealt with and removed, health and happiness will return.

We had known these folks for some time through our ministry travels. Their pastor was a dear friend, and we respected his counsel. This family in his church we had grown to love. A husband, wife, and their two sons. The sons were older, in their late teens, and both had minor problems with the law. Teenage stuff, not drugs or alcohol problems, I don't think, or that we knew about anyway. Each year we would go and minister at our friends' church, and they would say, "We want to come and help you at your Center." I would express my appreciation, but tell them it would be an extreme sacrifice on their part because they lived in another state, on the other side of the country. Nevertheless, each year they would say the same thing.

As our Center continued to grow, we needed more help and their offer sounded better and better. So we felt like we knew this couple and decided to accept their offer. I asked their pastor's advice and he said the younger of the two boys was constantly getting into trouble and the change would give him the opportunity to get a fresh start. The father was a handyman and could help me build and run the Center. The older boy was difficult too, but not as much as the younger boy. The mother would be a help to Sandy. The couple wanted to get a fresh start and sell their home and business, which was slowly diminishing.

So, I said, "Okay, let's try it for a year." We would pay their travel expenses for them to get to the Center, give them a place to stay, pay their utilities, and a small salary to help them. In a month they were ready and on their way.

Our Youth House was empty now. Our original caretakers found the work more difficult than they expected, especially after our first Youth leader's death. They had gotten involved with another church. This gave us a place to put this family. I felt it was God's open door for them. We were able to raise the money for their travel expenses, and I believed all was falling into place

Pulling into the center in their car and a U-Haul with all their things, they were overjoyed with their new home and to be part of God's work with us. We were just as excited to see them. The father was such a great help to me building things and helping me run the Youth Center. The mother was also a help to Sandy. However, many times she would allow her kids to do things we were trying to break our street kids from doing. We had hoped she would see the benefit and reasoning for our teaching and encourage her two sons to follow along.

"Love" was always the explanation she used to explain away their allowing the boys to ignore the rules. Others at the Center we asked did adhere to the rules and our authority and were better for it. Watch out when people keep bringing up what a loving God we have when it comes to overlooking sin and rebellion. God does love us unconditionally, but that does not give us the license to sin or go against His servants He puts in authority.

A few months went by, and many times their boys would skip church on Sunday. The Youth House was only one hundred feet from the sanctuary, not very hard to get to service. The times they missed, their mother would tell me they were sick or overslept. Yep, those excuses only go so far, unless you are emphasizing the "Love" factor.

I first brought it to the attention of the father, who was supposed to be the head of the house. He simply said he would talk to them. After talking to him, God quickly brought to my mind His word in **1 Timothy 3:5 "For if a man does not know how to rule his own house, how will he take care of the church of God?" NKJV**

A little more time passed and there was no change in their behavior. I called their former pastor and explained the situation. He said, "I was hoping the change would give them an opportunity to get a fresh start working with you and God's work. We had the same problem here, and I am afraid if they don't make it there, they are in for some trouble." I told him I would give it a few more weeks.

I went over one morning with donuts, they are always a good comfort food, and sat down with both parents and explained that our kids were watching them and asking why they had to follow the rules, but their boys didn't? I explained we try to teach the kids that by honoring God, He honors them. One thing I emphasized was always attending church on Sunday, keeping it a day of Sabbath to honor God, and never working on Sunday to keep the Sabbath day holy. If they learn this simple practice now as children, it will bless them when they are adults. I used scriptures to explain this was God's plan and not mine. They agreed, and we prayed for their boys. Yeah, score one for God, I thought.

I was out of town ministering and raising funds when I got a call from Sandy. She had done the service that Sunday morning, and we had the father do the service for me Sunday night. She said she noticed the younger of the two boys wasn't in service that morning and asked the mother why. She said he wasn't feeling well so he stayed home. Sandy just accepted her explanation and moved on.

After Sunday evening service was over, Sandy and Dominick Jr. decided to stop at the drive up window, at one of the prominent fast food places in town, to get a couple of milkshakes. What!!! Guess who was the happy and healthy window attendant? Yep, you guessed it, the younger son that was supposed to be home sick in bed. The Bible says your sin will find you out. "Bingo!" It didn't take long. Sandy called and informed me of the situation.

We don't give up easy on people; that's probably why God called us to such a hard work. Arriving home, a couple of days later, I wrote in a letter to them of what we expected so there would be no more confusion. The rules were so simple, attend church on Sunday, do not work on God's holy day, and be a good Christian example to those we are reaching for Jesus. I sent a copy to their former pastor so he would know I was doing my best. They immediately went to one of my Board Members in town and wanted him to get me to change the rules for them and they scheduled a meeting at his home. At the meeting I could tell I had lost this battle and soon their spirit would infect this Board Member. That's the way the devil works, many times from within.

The following week I received a handwritten, hand-delivered letter by the father, saying they cannot live up to such hard rules and they would be leaving in two weeks. I didn't feel badly about their choice, as a matter of fact, *I felt good*. God was moving them out.

Now none of them attended church or helped at the center in any way from that day on. That was fine with me. Our kids were growing and getting back on track not having conflicting examples to follow. I thought that was the hard part. "Not!"

"Oh, God please don't ask me to do this," I begged. "Why?" "They are leaving of their own free will, I didn't ask them to leave," I said. What was He asking me to do? It was a Friday and they were scheduled to leave first thing that following Monday. I woke up around 3:00 A.M.

and God said, "I want you to wash their feet before they leave and give them a good send off." A custom rarely done in churches today.

I couldn't go back to sleep. I had only done this once before at a foot washing service we had for Easter week and that was a joyous, awesome experience. The person's feet I washed got saved and set free from the pain he had felt since the Viet Nam war. This would be another thing altogether.

I can't tell you how hard this was. I have faced knives in my face, threats of bodily harm by bar owners, gang threats, but nothing compared to this. I knew if I didn't do this, God would not know when He would be able to trust me to follow His leading again. God will ask you to do some hard things in your life, but they will all work out for your good, if you are called according to His purpose.

Many people think ministry is a fun easy way of life. They don't realize it takes much sacrifice, but with that sacrifice God sends much reward. It is better for people who want to do something for God to just send in financial support to those He has called to serve Him full time than to try and live a life they were not called to live.

I arrived at 7:00 A.M. the next day with donuts and woke everybody up at the Youth House. Boxes were piled everywhere, ready to be filled with things that were just unpacked a few months ago. The two adults came downstairs to the living room, but the boys refused and wouldn't get out of bed. Sitting on the couch the mother and father asked what this was all about. I told them what God had told me to do. I wanted to send them off with His blessing and wash their feet. "No, no way," they said. "I understand, but I want you to know I appreciate all you have done here to help and pray you find what you are looking for back home," I said.

I'm no saint, and this is not what I wanted to do or what I was feeling in my heart, but I was going to be obedient to the One I serve.

So, they said they would allow me to wash their feet, but not the boys. I said okay, I didn't want to press my luck and you can't make people do what they don't want to do. After all, these were "Professing

Christians," and I'm sure they wanted to appear that way to me. Imagine Christ washing Judas's feet knowing he would betray Him?

Remember, He said, **"You are clean, but not all of you." John 13:10 NKJV**

I filled a bucket with warm water and grabbed a towel from the kitchen. I must confess at that point I wanted to use cold water, but that wouldn't be Christ-like, so I asked forgiveness and went about my task.

The father just sat there and let me do it with no emotion. He was receptive to what I was trying to do and just admitted this work was much more difficult than he had expected. Now it was time to wash the mother's feet.

It was a struggle. As I began to pray she kept pulling her feet out of the water. Her spirit was so hostile, and she could not look me in the face. It was obvious God was exposing the root of the problem. The water was warm, but the room was filled with a coldness you could not miss. My task done I left quickly and went back home.

That following Monday they left and refused the prayer of safe travel we offered them. I received a call from their former pastor saying he understood and knew I had done my best. Their pastor was once again doing the best he could for them. I thank God for exposing what only He could see.

Your walk many times will not be easy, but it will always be blessed, if you do not faint and walk His way.

Chapter Twenty-Five (Triumph)

> ***"For I have chosen him, so that he will direct his children and his household after him to keep the way of the Lord by doing what is right and just, so that the Lord will bring about for Abraham what he has promised him." Genesis 18:19 NIV***

Cleaning my office, one day, I came across a card I had placed on my office shelf of special things. I use these very special things to reflect on during times of testing and stress. I had just gone through one of those times. I sat there at my desk watching my printer do things I didn't know it could do, and I grabbed this card. It was given to me by our son Dominick Jr., on Father's Day, with a poem in it written by Amy Matayo.

Taking this moment to myself I read:

"There are many examples to follow in life, many men who are deserving of praise. Whether doctors, or lawyers, or soldiers of war, they're given in so many ways. But of all of the men who've accomplished it all, all of the great leaders we've had, not one will ever begin to compare, with my Dad. He's taught me his values, he's raised me with love, he's always shown me his respect; and though his name may never appear in bright lights, he's one man you'd never forget. My Dad is my leader, my pattern for life, and on him I can surely depend. For I know he will be there with arms open wide to be my example, my friend." It was like my son was there saying, "You are His good example to me, Dad." Isn't it amazing how God sends encouragement from the most unexpected places? A little card I cherished for so many years touched and healed my broken spirit that day.

In our world today children have very few Christian role models to look up to. They have basketball stars who dress like women and get AIDS from having pre-marital sex. They have pro boxers who punch out their wives. They have TV and Film heroes who are just as vile as the villains they are after. We have women who say it is normal to marry other women and men having sex with men. Our children have gangs for families, because the gangs are always there for each other, whereas the parents are too busy or gone.

Jesus made it easy for us to do something for Him. We don't need to have a lot of money. We don't need to have a lot of free time. All we need to do is be *His* example to our children.

The Apostles watched everything Jesus did. They listened to everything Jesus said. We may not realize it, but our children are doing the same with us. We as the adults are the greatest examples in life they will see. We are the ones they see get out of bed in the morning. They see how we react throughout the course of the day. When they lay their heads on their pillows at night, we are the last voice they will hear before they drift off to sleep.

We can't tell our children to do one thing as we do another. Christ never preached a sermon He didn't live. We who are called Christians, "Followers of Christ," must do the same. It is our responsibility.

Going back to my "special shelf" to put back the card I had just relished, I found another of Dominick Jr.'s cards I had kept, with another poem by an unknown author.

"Walk a little plainer Daddy, said the little boy so frail, I'm following in your footsteps and I do not want to fail. Sometimes your steps are very plain, sometimes they are hard to see, so walk a little plainer daddy, for you are leading me. I know that once you walked this way many years ago, and what you did along the way I'd really like to know. For sometimes when I am tempted I don't know what to do, so walk a little plainer daddy for I must follow you. Someday when I'm grown up, you are like what I want to be, then I will have a little boy who will want to follow me. And I would want to lead him right and help him to be true, so walk a little plainer daddy, for we must follow you."

Chapter Twenty-Six (Triumph)

"You will be brought before governors and kings for My sake, as a testimony to them and to the gentiles." Matthew 18:18 NKJV

The city was taking notice of our work now. There was no way they could deny the impossible was happening. They knew I had no stash of money somewhere that I could draw on—well, those who checked into me or really knew me did. There would always be the gossip that I had plenty of money from my "Showbiz" days. When God is in a work, He gets you noticed, and we got noticed by a man who would come along side me, become my friend, and be used by God greatly for this work.

We had become friends with many in the Methodist Church after the "Musical Salute to America" benefit raising money for the basketball court for the children. A lady in the church who was a retired school teacher, never married, and lived with her sister contacted me.

"Reverend Farone, how are you doing today?" she said. "Oh hi, just fine, how are you?" I asked. "I'm excited," she said. "I have someone that wants to meet you, are you busy right now?" "Well, no, I'm just sitting in my office contemplating the day," I replied. "Good, we will be right over," she said and hung up the phone.

Minutes later she came walking into the little Christian Shop with a very distinguished older gentleman. My office was just off the hallway that led to our main sanctuary so getting up from my desk I went to hug her and greet him. "Pastor Nick, I'd like you to meet my nephew who I have told all about you and your work. This is former Governor Dave C. Treen of Louisiana," she said.

"I've been looking forward to meeting you, young man," he said. "I want you to know you are doing a great work for the children of this city and Louisiana, and I want to do whatever I can to help you." "This is such an honor, sir," I said. "This dear lady never told me she had such a distinguished nephew." "We're just family, and I consider you family now too," he said. "Nick, would you show me around a bit? I'd like to see your place and find out what I can do to help," he continued.

I proceeded to take him on the thirty minute tour through all the buildings and share the vision I had back in 1995. I found out he had expertise in grant writing and the contacts interested in helping where they could. He went right to work.

Things didn't change quickly, as most of the time they don't, but they were changing. This fellow gave us the infusion of excitement and hope we all needed. We had eight regulars working with us now. Working very hard trying to keep up with running the Youth Center, running the Youth House, running the Christian Shop, doing services on Sunday, gutting and rebuilding the old bar hoping to turn it into a restaurant, getting playground equipment, and putting up fences around our main properties. We had our hands full. But there was always another need...

One of our girls came into the Youth Center and said, "Pastor Nick, you-know-who is taking a dump by the tree again." Argh! I ran out to the familiar spot he had found for his private potty break.

"Heyyyyyyy! You only live down the street, why are you pooping here?" I had to keep from laughing. I knew why. He didn't want to go home and get stuck there doing something with his brothers or around

Inside Youth Center games

Playground

drug dealers and drunks. "I'm sorry, Pastor Nick, I won't do it again," he said. He quickly pulled up his pants and ran back to the Youth center.

"God," I said, "I need so much I can't raise enough to cover all this and I have been faithful with what I have, but You know the need," then I went back to the Youth Center to be monitor/referee.

The first thing our new friend did was get us a grant for the Youth Center and money for new games and the toilets to be put in so poo poo kid didn't have to poo poo behind the tree anymore. We also got beds for the Youth House and playground equipment.

Governor Treen and I started having lunch frequently at a favorite restaurant nearby where he lived in south Louisiana. We would catch each other up to date on the progress at the Center, and he honored me by joining my Board of Directors.

One day he called me and said, "Nick, I know this is last minute but, can you come down to Baton Rouge tomorrow? My friend, former President George Bush Sr., will be speaking to 500 people at a private dinner and I'd like you to join me." I think before he hung up his phone I was there at his house!

It was so exciting entering the hotel ballroom where the event was being held. Secret Service agents were everywhere. Security dogs smelled each one of us as we entered the ballroom. One lingered at me for a moment, which made me a little nervous. Then I remembered I must have the scent of our dogs on me from leaving home, riding in the car, and picking off their hairs from my newly pressed suit. I was okay; they let me pass.

Seated at one of the best tables, close to the front, I looked around the room. It was filled with Congressmen, Mayors, Senators, and one regular person, me. Sitting there with my friend, who left me by myself as he was invited up to the front to join a select group, I was in awe. Reflecting for a moment I thought, "Look at where God has brought me." I didn't feel I deserved to be there with all these great men and women who are in positions to change the world. "Oh man! Look, I just spilled my water on the table, very good impression you're making, Nick," then I stopped talking to myself.

The President entered the room to a standing ovation as we all applauded and then sat down. He spoke about the need to reach the next generation for our country. My thoughts exactly, but mine went a little further. We needed to reach them for Christ.

After his speech, President Bush left the room and a spokesperson came to the podium. "Please listen closely, we know many of you here have asked to have a private audience with the President, but his time is very limited and he has chosen only twelve that he will be able to see. The President apologizes and appreciates your understanding," he said and left the room.

Still enjoying the time at my table waiting for my friend to return, I just thought I would relax and soak in the moment. Coming out of the same door the President had exited only moments before, I saw my friend coming towards our table. I got up thinking it was time to leave. "Nick, come with me. The President wants to meet you," he said. I couldn't believe my ears, but I heard correctly. I jumped up, brushed off the remaining dog hairs from my pants, and followed him into a back room off the ballroom.

There he was, the President of the United States, standing on the left, half way into the room. We were in a line that was supervised by his aides, to let us know when it was our time to go meet him.

"So where's this miracle man you wrote me about?" the President shouted across the room to my friend who turned around and pointed to me. I turned around and looked behind me. "Here he is," Governor Treen said as he escorted me up to the President.

"This is such an honor for me, Mr. President, to meet you, but I'm no miracle man. If it weren't for Jesus, none of this would be happening," I said. "I have a letter about what you are doing right here in my jacket pocket," he said as he reached into his coat and pulled out the letter my friend wrote. "I want to tell you that you are doing a much needed work in our country and to keep it up," President Bush said.

"Thank you, sir, so very much," I said. We shook hands, had our picture taken together, and I went to leave.

On the way out the same door we had entered, I heard someone yell, "Nick!" It was the President. "Keep up the good work," he said as he patted his jacket pocket. "I will, Mr. President," I said as we left the room. Here I was, just someone who made a choice to trust God and His promises, and look at where He's brought me. I am very humbled.

Me, President Bush, Gov. Treen

Chapter Twenty-Seven (Triumph)

> ***"Honor the Lord with your possessions, And with the first fruits of all your increase." Proverbs 3:9 NKJV***

It was 1998, and we had been hard at work restoring the old bar and needed to keep vandals from destroying our progress. What we needed to do was to put a fence around that property to protect it. Where could I get the money? What could I sell? The local Sheriff had seen the change we were making with the youth in the city and submitted me for an **Angel Award with the Louisiana Blue Cross Blue Shield Foundation** for working with underprivileged kids. Out of 150 submissions, they would pick eight. *There's that number again*!

We were one of the eight they chose, and we received a check for $2,500.00 for our work. The fence cost $2,400.00, so I had it installed right away and I didn't have to do it myself. The prophecy of the watch was coming true.

Chapter Twenty-Eight (Trial)

"He will swallow up death forever, And the Lord God will wipe away tears from all faces." Isaiah 25:8 NKJV

There have been many special people brought into our lives to help us build God's work. Two were my Uncle George and Aunt Ginny. George had passed on, and Ginny was about to go and be with him, so I made a trip to my old hometown, Schenectady, NY, to see her.

Sitting at her bedside in the hospital the nurses gave her a little time for visitors. "Well, I heard you are going to be with George soon and I just wanted to come and be with you before you left," I said. Her hand was so frail and soft as I held it. Looking from her chipped polished fingernails up to her sweet gentle face, I saw one of God's precious angels. Her hair was much thinner now, and there were age lines around her eyes that still had the dried tears from her morning's sleep in them. The nurses had told me she could no longer eat or even open her eyes. Her communication had been reduced to little screams, and they weren't sure if she would wake up.

Looking at her fragile figure resting before me, I knew she would very soon be leaving this natural body and receiving her beautiful spiritual body to join her husband, George. My mind was flooded with all the good times we had spent together, and I began to reminisce and talk with my beloved aunt Ginny

"I remember the time we were sitting there talking around the breakfast table and George turned to show me something out the window, when he turned back to grab his cup, you had taken it, washed it, and already put it in the cupboard. 'Boy she's fast,' George said as he broke into laughter that lasted for about ten minutes."

I sat there sharing the good old days for about twenty minutes when all of a sudden I felt a squeeze on my hand and one eye opened. Raising my hand to her lips, she kissed it, and said, "I love you." "Nurse, nurse come quick," I called out. The nurse came into the room, and I asked Ginny if she knew who I was. "Sure," she said clearly. She began to respond to some of the stories I continued to tell.

"Remember, like the time we were pulled over by the State Police in Mississippi when they thought Sandy and I were bank robbers?" she smiled. Her laughter wasn't that deep laugh she used to have; it was more like a little scream of delight. It was music to my ears.

After about an hour, I had to leave, hospital regulations. I told her I'd see her in the morning, knowing full well she could be with George by then. Back in my room that night, I couldn't help but thank God for the special gift He gave me.

The next morning, when I arrived at the hospital, I couldn't believe my eyes. I walked into the room, and there was Aunt Ginny sitting up in bed. Her eyes were wide open, and she was smiling at me. "She's had a good meal and she's doing much better," the nurse said to me. "She's alert and we are just going to give her a bath," she continued. "Good morning, Aunt Ginny, you look wonderful!" I said taking her hand again. She pulled it up to her mouth, kissed it, and said, "I love you." I asked her if she had eaten anything and she said, "Yes."

As I was talking to her, my Uncle Joe came into the room and stood at the foot of the bed. He was amazed. "She doesn't know me," he said. "Aunt Ginny, do you know who this is?" I asked her. "Sure," she said. My Uncle Joe came closer. "Ginny, do you know who I am?" he said.

"SURE," she said more emphatically, "Joe." We stayed and had a nice visit. The rest of the family came in to visit with her over the next couple of days. I knew Aunt Ginny was ready to go and be with George, but I didn't know how much time God would give her. My prayer was, when God did take her home, it would be peaceful.

On December 21, 1998, Ginny was reunited with George, after drifting off to sleep. She is once again stealing his coffee cup as he points to one of God's glorious creations.

We may be very busy in our chosen lifestyles, but we must always remember, if we are too busy for God and the ones He has blessed us with, we are too busy. God honors us when we take the time for Him and others.

Chapter Twenty-Nine (Triumph)

> ***"Give and it will be given to you: good measure, pressed down, shaken together, and running over will be put into your bosom. For with the same measure that you use, it will be measured back to you." Luke 6:38 NKJV***

It was Palm Sunday and I was invited to Maumelle, AR. to do services for friends.

We had met them in the early years of our ministry as we traveled on the evangelistic road. They were new to the ministry, excited, and young. I will never forget this miracle.

We were living week to week on our Sunday service offerings and needing gas and food for the upcoming week. We entered the small church sanctuary on that Sunday morning of about twenty people, and Nicky (Dominick Jr.) ran around shaking everyone's hands, as was his custom. We had dinner with our new friends the night before, at their home. It was a nice home that was provided for them by the church.

I gave my testimony through music and the word that morning, as I usually did, and the people were generous. The offering came to $200.00. During the service, the pastor was informed that there had been an electrical fire in the air-conditioning unit at their home. All was okay, but you could tell they were discouraged. The church was a church that was supported by the State office for six months. That meant they would send $150.00 a week to the pastor to help his family with their personal needs. That time of support was coming to an end.

I had a thought and shared it with Sandy. "Why don't we take a step of faith and give the offering back to help this young couple?" We were in a campground that was already paid for, the owner of the campground brought over some fresh vegetables for us, and all we really needed was gas money to get to our next place of ministry. When I presented the idea to Sandy she agreed. So we gave the offering back. We didn't tell anyone.

That night someone came to my service, and when they left they gave me a "Pentecostal Handshake." That means they put $100.00 in my hand as they left. God provided the gas money we needed. He was honoring our sacrifice, but I didn't know how much until years later...

Now here we are many years later, with the same couple doing a service for them, in a new state, over a pizza shop. They were joined by another church and were in the midst of building a new church for a church planting and were meeting there temporarily.

Before the service, I was standing outside the door to their sanctuary, on the second floor, and just looking out the window at their parking lot. Parked there I saw an old 1963 Grey bus that looked like it had just been repainted. Talking to God I said, "Now that's what we need for the kids, God. That would be perfect to take our Mission trips in." Then I went in to the sanctuary to get ready for service.

After I finished my part of the service, the pastor got up and said, "Someone heard Pastor Nick talking about our bus we just had refinished, and brought it to my attention. I have an idea. We don't really have any kids right now that we can use it for, so why don't we give it to his ministry for their kids?" I was awestruck again.

"Tell you what, let's do," he continued. "Next Sunday is Easter, let's pray about giving it to them during the week and take a vote next Sunday," then he finished with a prayer and we all went out for a nice meal.

The following Easter Sunday, I got a call from the pastor. "Well, the vote was unanimous, come on up and get your bus. We also put in a new battery for you, so it's all yours," he said. God had taken a $200.00 investment into His servants years earlier and turned it into a bus we needed now.

You can't out-give God, for those of you who are afraid God will not repay your trust and generous giving to Him and His work. He always blesses giving, especially sacrificially. My first book, *Faith How It Works*, and this book are true testimonies to His promises.

Chapter Thirty (Trial)

> ***And God spoke all these words saying; "I am the Lord your God who brought you out of the land of Egypt, out of the house of bondage. "You shall have no other gods before Me." Exodus 20:1-3***

Sometimes in our lives we will go through situations and circumstances we don't understand. Particularly when in the natural everything looks good and positive. There are things God sees and knows that are hurting us, that we don't see, and He will reveal Himself to us in order to keep us moving in the right direction.

I had noticed a change in some of our young people at the Center. Some of the children who would run up and give us hugs weren't doing so anymore. I couldn't put my finger on it, but something was different. I noticed the spirit of rebellion in some of the adults, and the children were picking it up too. Not just the normal fighting I was used to, but a real competitiveness. I even noticed that some of the adults who had been most helpful at the Center began to question every new change God was doing. What was it?

As I walked around the Youth Center straightening up chairs and tables, I spoke to God. "Things seem to be going so wonderfully and yet there is something wrong, I can feel it." I said. Then it dawned on me. We had instituted a new program to give the Youth an incentive to attend the Center. If our Youth attended service on Sundays faithfully, worked at the Center doing small projects to help out (one day a month), kept their grades up in school, we would provide free karate classes. Someone from out of town had offered to give the kids their classes free of charge.

There were about fifteen to start, including some of our volunteer adults, and the class size was growing. After five months the person decided to open their own school in town and left our kids flat. They no longer would come to the Center for our kids for free.

As I was putting the puzzles back in their shelves I prayed, "God, should I try to find someone else to continue these classes for the kids here who are coming to church and growing in Your word?" I heard His voice say, "Dominick," He always calls me Dominick, "This place was never meant to be a place of violence." It was almost as if someone had turned a light on.

Putting the foosh-ball game back to its original spot that had been vacant to make room for the class, I remembered how the kids loved to play that game. I even thought of getting another one when we had the money. I then realized the difference there was of playing a game of basketball, pool, foosh-ball, or checkers, to training to compete one against another in physical combat.

In my days of Soap Opera acting, I used to take karate to release all the pent up anxiety I had from that pressured-filled world I lived in. Now with the Lord in my life, He gave me the release of the tension I was looking for.

Putting back the puzzle table, coloring table, and Miss Pac-Man game, the lights in the room seemed to get brighter when I took down the karate flag that was up every week for class. I could also sense freshness in the air, almost like someone opened a window. I know this sounds strange, but that is exactly what it felt like.

When I walked out the front door, with garbage bags in hand, my Lord spoke and said, "Look up, what does that say?" I looked up and read, “Christian Youth Center.” Then His inner voice said, “It does not say karate center. This is a place of fellowship not fighting.”

Walking over to plug in our youth sign for the night, the same voice said, “Look up, what does that sign say?” It was a list of the original activities planned for the Center. They focused on fellowship and Christian service, and karate was not in that list. “This place, My place, is for fellowship with Me and each other,” God said, and He opened my eyes to the change I had seen.

The next day we were having lunch with some friends at their lovely home, and I shared my experience with them. “Nick, I’ve done some extensive research on ancient Asian religions and things that have grown out of their background,” she said. Being she ministers overseas quite a bit, I wanted to hear what she had to say.

“The art of karate is one of those things that came out of ancient Asian religions. It is more than a thousand years old and originated in eastern Asia, a godless nation. First, as a monastic training and later as a defense method used by Chinese peasants against armed bandits. Eventually it moved to Japan and Korea. You have dedicated your Christian Youth center to God and His service. Buddha, Hinduism, and other religions are gods of darkness and death. Jesus is the true God of life and light. You, unknowingly, wanting to do something for the children to build their self esteem, moral character, and positive attitude, brought something in direct competition to God’s character. Satan is very cunning and deceptive and even himself comes as an angel of light.” ***2 Corinthians 11:14*** **“And no wonder! For Satan himself transforms himself into an angel of light.”** ***NKJV***

She was so right. God’s word tells us that we were once in darkness, but now we are in the light and we are to walk as children of the light.

In the U.S., karate has become a highly popular sport and method of self protection. It has been incorporated into training programs for police, soldiers, and college athletes. It does have its place. However, at our Center we intended to develop Christian character, love, and fellowship. That was our goal. That was our mission.

Sometimes there are things in our lives we don't realize are affecting us and all appears well on the surface. God will bring to light those things He wants us to see, so we can make our own choice to walk as children of Light.

Chapter Thirty-One (Triumph)

"And my God shall supply all your need according to His riches in glory by Christ Jesus." Philippians 4:19 NKJV

Shortly after that realization God would use my friend's walking tour through the main building again to bless us. The Governor saw the ceilings were all damaged from a leaking roof and the parking lots were all covered with pot holes from where the black top had eroded over the many years. He contacted the Foundations, of which he was one of their Board members, and told them of our needs. Soon we received a large grant to put on a new roof and resurfaced the two parking lots. It was another day of celebration for His kids. God wasn't through yet...

Sitting in my office, I was marveling at what God was doing with very little. Our very little was growing into very much, all through prayer and faith. Ring! ring! ring! "Hello, this is Nick Farone, who's calling?" "This is so-and-so and I'm calling from Missouri. You don't know me, but my mother lives there in your city. She recently moved there, and I will be joining her soon. The reason I'm calling is, she has some ceramic molds and two kilns she wants to donate to your Center. All you have to do is come pick them up before I move there," the lady said.

"Well, I'm afraid I don't have the capability to come to Missouri and get them, but thank you so much for your generous offer," I said. "By the way, how many molds are we talking about?" I asked. "Two thousand or so," she said. "Two thousand!" I said. "Yes, my mother has a lot of them, plus two kilns," she said. "Oh my, let me see if I can figure something out and I'll get back to you," I said.

Sitting there thinking an idea came to mind. I'll act as if. What does that mean you say? I play this mental game. I ask myself, "What if I had all the money I needed to make this happen? I will act as if I do and figure out a way to get them."

That's blind faith. You prepare, even though you have no way to make something happen. You act as if you do. I started calling truck rental places and getting prices. I found that with the truck rental and gas, it would cost about $1,000.00 to make the trip. I didn't have $1,000.00, so what would I do?

Light Bulb!

I did have a Christian TV program and a $500.00 watch I had put away for safekeeping. What if I went on TV and said I would give this $500.00 watch to anyone who would give me $1,000.00 cash to make this trip? That way they would be matching my $500.00 investment with their $500.00 investment and I would have the money. Pretty cool idea! So I presented it to the TV station owner, and he thought it was a great idea.

On that Tuesday night I went on the air live and said, "I will give this $500.00 gold watch to anyone who gives me $1,000.00 cash for this need." Within ten minutes the TV station received a call and the person said they would be up in the morning to the Christian Shop with the money.

Around 10:00 A.M. the next morning a man walked into the Christian Shop and asked to speak with me. Walking up to the counter he said, "Here's your $1,000.00" and proceeded to put ten $100.00 bills on the counter. "Thank you so very much, sir, what's your name?" I asked. "That's not important," he said, "Here's the money for the kids."

"Well, I can't thank you enough," I said, "Here's your watch, enjoy it, and remember it as a witness to what you did for God's kids." We shook hands and he walked out. I went back to my office and immediately started making the arrangements to rent the truck.

About twenty minutes had passed and the man came back into Sandy's shop. I saw him coming and went out to greet him. "Hello again," I said. "I've already booked the truck and we will be on our way to pick up the molds and kilns next week. Thank you again so much."

"I want to give you another gift, in memory of my wife," he said. "We used to watch you every week together on the Christian station and you blessed us with your singing." As he said that, he took the watch off and gave it back to me. We both teared up and I couldn't say anything. I went around the counter and hugged him and then he left. As he was getting into his car, a still small voice said to me, **"I told you, you would never have to sell the watch**."

God wasn't done yet. Arriving to pick up the molds and kilns I found there were 3,000 molds, not 2,000. Good thing I rented the bigger truck.

Chapter Thirty-Two (Triumph)

> ***"Bring all the tithes into the storehouse, That there may be food in My house, And try Me now in this," Says the Lord of hosts, "If I will not open for you the windows of heaven, And pour out for you such blessing, That there will not be room enough to receive it." Malachi 3:10 NKJV***

"Stuff," we had stuff! It had been a few years now since I had my vision in 1995, but little by little, it was all becoming reality. We owned and were working on all the properties, except the State Building. That building was still being used by the Motor Vehicle Dept, and to tell you the truth, I had all I could handle.

We had continued to work on the old bar, but we still needed all the things it would take to make it a restaurant. Kitchen equipment, tables, chairs, bathrooms, grease hood, all still needed to be installed. We also needed a sign of some kind on the restaurant building to let people know it was a restaurant. These needs alone would cost $57,000.00.

The Youth Center needed central heating and air-conditioning. We had ceiling fans in the summer time, but they were not enough to keep the place cool. In the winter, it would get too cold in there. That would cost another $10,000.00.

Our 1963 bus was seeing its better days and not handling the long trips well anymore. I had seen a used forty-six passenger tour bus, on sale for $30,000.00, yeah right. These were long-term needs, and we were thankful for what we had and how far we had come from our humble beginnings.

Something we taught our kids, right from the beginning, was to be faithful in tithing and giving. God always honors giving to His work. We started when our offerings were only $4.36 on a Sunday. Now sometimes our offerings would be a couple of thousand dollars from out-of-town givers. When we started we would give our tithe to the Christian TV station that helped us many times promote what we were doing. Each year the owner of the station would give a dinner for all the supporters and plaques of appreciation to each one. There were three big plaques given to the top three givers for the year, and it seemed the same big church got the biggest one each year for first place. "Wow, Pastor Nick, look at that one! How can we get that one?" one of our little ones said to me at dinner. We took our kids with us many times to the event because none of them ever had a dinner like this. "I tell you what, someday we will get the biggest plaque because we will always give God His money and He sees our hearts," I said.

Year after year our giving/tithe increased to the station. We moved to third place and then second place. But never first place...The big church always won, it was almost expected.

One day Sandy was handing out bubble gum to the kids, after school, as they came to her Christian Shop. It was her daily ritual that she loved and looked forward to. Someone else entered her shop this day. It was a man, I would say in his late seventies, came walking in with a cane. His left foot was bandaged and he came through the parking lot door. "Excuse me, is Reverend Farone here? I'd like to talk with him if he's not busy," he said.

I came out of my office and walked up to him. "Hello, I'm Nick Farone, what can I do for you?" "My name is Clarke, and I wanted to have a look around your place to see if you had any needs I could help with," he said. That name sounded familiar, but I couldn't place it at the time. "Sure, I'd be happy to show you around," I said.

We walked as far as the end of the basketball court where you could see the Youth Center, the future restaurant, the Youth House, and the main Building. Stretching out my arms I said, "Pick one." I was joking, but not really. I didn't want to make him walk all around the place with his bandaged foot. Through our conversation I found out he just had toe surgery and felt he would appreciate not having to go through doors, up stairs, and over play areas. He was appreciative and stopped right there. He looked at me and said, "If the good Lord doesn't take me home, I'll have a check in the mail to help you out by Friday." We shook hands and I walked him back to his car.

Many people say, "The check is in the mail." So I just said thank you and left it at that. Still, something was familiar about him, even though we had never met before. When you rely on your donations every day, it's disappointing when folks forget you or think they will catch up some time. Most of the time, they never do. They just assume God will touch someone else to do it.

On Friday there was only one envelope in the mail and it was from my mystery visitor. I opened it and fell back in my chair. It was a check for $100,000.00. Yes, that's what I said, $100,000.00. It dawned on me who he was. He was one of the three owners of the funeral home who donated it to us. I called him immediately at his office to thank him. "That's all right," he said, "You just keep up the good work," and he hung up the phone.

That's exactly what we did. We got everything we needed to finish the restaurant, put the air-conditioning/heating unit in the Youth Center, and bought the forty-six passenger bus for our travels. We also donated our other bus to a mission work in Nicaragua. God honored that too, and some of our Prayer Partners sent in special offerings, unsolicited.

This year, at the TV Station dinner, guess who won first prize in their giving? Yep, a bunch of street kids who had given faithfully from what they had received over the past eight years. "*First prize this year goes to New Beginnings Christian Center*," the owner said with great delight. The big church was shocked, but happy to come in second.

Chapter Thirty-Three (Trial/Blessing)

"And we know that all things work together for good to those who love God, to those who are called according to His purpose." Romans 8:28 NKJV

I have found, over the course of my life, that God will many times take a terrible situation and turn it into a magnificent blessing. One of the best things we can do for ourselves is to journal. Some call this practice "Keeping a Diary." I guess you could look at it that way. It's like writing a diary to someone who will always love you, never judge you, and who will always be there to comfort and listen to you.

It was the Wednesday before "Good Friday" in 2001, and we had just been given three goats to mow our lawn. Yes, that's what I said, "Three goats." Their names were Romeo, Juliet, and Lancelot. "Let me splain...," as it was once said in a movie.

The grass at the Center would grow so quickly it would constantly need to be mowed. We didn't have the funds to hire someone every two weeks to cut it, and some friends gave us a suggestion. "Nick, what you need are some goats to keep your lawn mowed for you at the Center, and we have three we will drop off for you to try out." "Okay,"

I said, "Why not?" I thought they might be great fun for the kids and cure my grass problem to boot.

That Wednesday they arrived and went right to work at their job. Thursday they had already eaten a great deal of the grass, and the kids were overjoyed with their new pets. Yeah!!!

Early on "Good Friday" morning I went to the Center to start getting things ready for our "Easter Sunrise Service" that was coming up Sunday. Pulling into the parking lot by the Youth Center, I didn't see our new arrivals at their work in the playground.

Parking the van I walked over to the gate and saw a horrific sight. Romeo and Juliet lay dead and Lancelot stood by them a little bloodied. "Oh God, what has happened? Who did this to our goats?" We had faced many attacks at the Center from some in the community who just didn't want us there. Who would be so cruel as to do this?

Walking over to Lancelot he let me pet him, though I could see he was shaken. Looking past him to our fence I saw it was still intact, but under it was a huge hole that had been dug out to gain entry. There was some fur on the bottom of the fence that would explain this catastrophe. My immediate concern was to get Romeo and Juliet out and Lancelot back to his home safely.

The city workers across the street, who arrived to work early, came to my rescue and helped me with Romeo and Juliet. Nicky and I got our Camp-mobile and took Lancelot back home and explained what had happened to our friends.

As we were trying to get Lancelot into our "Camp-mobile" I heard a whimpering under one of the bushes. Taking a moment to investigate, Nicky and I found a little puppy who was no more than two months old.

He was lying by an ear that had been ripped off one of the goats. He appeared to be guarding it. Reaching in gently under the bush, I lifted him out and into our lives.

What had happened, I found out later, was a pack of dogs came through the neighborhood and dug their way under our fence to get to the goats. This little two-month-old Border Collie was left behind as the pack left and guess he decided to stay behind and protect the goats, as best he could, by his in-bred nature.

We took him home and to our veterinarian. We found he was very sick with worms. Our dear friends there nursed him back to health. Little did I know at the time that God would use this little guy, ten years later, to become my best buddy, protector, and companion to face the most difficult three years and nine months of my life. That story is told a little later on in this book. Oh, and by the way, "Shakespeare," the name we gave him which we felt was appropriate, is still at my side as I write his chapter in my book.

Chapter Thirty-Four (Triumph)

"And the King will answer and say to them, "Assuredly, I say to you, inasmuch as you did it to one of the least of these My brethren, you did it to Me." Matthew 25:40

One of the mission trips we took our youth on was to the Navajo Indian Reservation and it held some surprises of the supernatural kind.

After years of Mexico mission trips, we decided to expand our kids' vision of Missions. The decision was made to take a missions trip of a different kind to an Indian mission. We joined another church and arrived at the reservation that was in the desert, a place called Pine Lake, New Mexico. Although, there was no lake there. The little shack-type houses people lived in were surrounded with goats and dogs all running loose. The goats they used for milk and to keep the brush areas pruned. The dogs, the Native Americans believe, keep the evil spirits known as "Skin Walkers" away.

In short the "Skin Walkers" are a legend the Native Americans believe. We were told when a certain level of maturity is reached, young men would go through a ritual where they enter a cave and come out possessed by the spirit of some animal, which guides them through life.

Each night, as we slept in our tents, we would hear the dogs carry on barking and then suddenly stop. One night we even saw an individual walking through the camp where our tents were. It was comforting to know, **"He who is in you is greater than he who is in the world." 1 John 4:4 NKJV**

The pastor on the reservation lived in a forty-foot mobile home. He, his wife, and two daughters had built the first church about fifteen years ago. Since then the church had added additions, roofs, and walls. They had a little chapel with a kitchen area attached where they ate and had fellowship after services.

Newly attached to that we saw our mission assignment for this trip ready and waiting. A concrete slab had been poured which was big enough to hold two complete bathrooms with showers and two classrooms. A pile of building materials lay waiting for us to get to work.

A few hundred yards from the house and about a hundred yards from the new slab stood two dilapidated and falling over outhouses. These were the community bathrooms. Even though we would be building two new indoor bathrooms, these two facilities would still be used quite a bit.

I walked over to see these sheds the children would be using daily and caught the aroma that was attracting our young people. "I ain't goin' in there," one said. "No way, I'll hold it for a week," another said. "I'll just go in the bushes," still another commented.

Viewing the first one-seater, with the hanging makeshift door and then walking over to the two-seater, with no door, I asked God what He wanted us to do. The team of men from the other church we went with jumped to work on the new building with all the new materials. We felt we would only get in their way. They were mostly professionals and already had a plan. It was like the Lord said, "I want you to restore the old outhouses."

I didn't understand why God wanted us to take these two terrible, smelly, and rotten buildings that should be torn down and rebuild them. It made no sense, especially since they would have brand new indoor bathrooms with running water soon. Nevertheless, this was what I felt He wanted us to do. Restoring buildings is what we had been doing for years at New Beginnings. I thought our youth would totally reject the idea, but they proved just the opposite. They were excited! "We are doing this for the Lord so let's build the best outhouses in the state of New Mexico," I said. "Let's make them something to be proud of."

So to work we went removing the old make shift door on one and tearing off the fallen roof on the other. It was exciting. Smelly, but exciting. Our boys and girls learned how to use a tape measure, skill saw, hammer and nails, power drill and screws. We even put a divider wall in the two-seater and double doors to give a little privacy. A door was added to the one-seater, and they both had privacy locks now on the inside.

A fifty pound bag of lye took care of the immediate smell. Then we vented the commodes with a vent pipe and fresh air vent. Toilet paper holders were the next upgrade and finally the finishing touch. Each outhouse was designed and painted by a collaboration of our youth.

They were painted bright white so you could see them from the road and the first thing you saw as you entered the camp. Then decorative rainbows, flowers, crosses and pictures were added to adorn the outside of these now lovely bathroom establishments.

During the building of the new inside bathrooms, these artistic creations were used by everyone in the camp throughout the day. One of the workers from the church we went with made fun of our efforts saying it was a waste of time and good lumber. But to see the pride on our kids' faces, knowing what they had done for Jesus, with their own hands, made it all worthwhile. Sure we didn't have the skills the professionals did. We didn't have the funds to build a $20,000.00 addition that was also being built to God's glory. But we did have the ability to use what we had and to do it to the best of our ability. It felt good!

That night there was a full moon, and in the desert you could see two shinning white outhouses, highlighted by its glow. This was much different from our first night there, trying to find the outhouses in the dark of night. It wasn't easy walking through dogs, cactus, trees, goat

TWO SEATER

pens, and old tires placed around the camp to keep the "Skin Walkers" away. Now they were like God's little prayer closets lighting the way.

As we rested in our tents, I heard the dogs barking. I got up to see what was causing them to bark like the night before. In the light of the moon I could see the figure of a man riding a horse. He had long hair and rode his horse just outside the circle of tires that were placed around the camp. The barking of the dogs made him ride off in another direction, so I went back to bed.

In the morning I went to the spot where I had seen the rider and looked for signs of hoof prints. There were none. I asked around to see if anyone else had seen him. They said they heard the dogs, but didn't look to see what they were barking at. I noticed that night the figure rode off in the opposite direction of our beautiful outhouses, adorned with rainbows, flowers, and *crosses*. There was no more need to put tires around the village for protection, as the Spirit of the Lord was now all they needed.

Oh, and one last thing I need to mention. There was some kind of tribal regulation that was not met putting in the septic tank for the new bathrooms, so *they were not allowed to be used. It took another two years to acquire to appropriate paperwork*, which meant our little outhouses were the only outhouses used during that time. God had us prepare them in advance.

Chapter Thirty-Five (Triumph)

"Delight yourself also in the Lord and He shall give you the desires of your heart." Psalm 37:4 NKJV

I hadn't seen my father in twenty-one years. It had been our son Dominick's prayer, ever since he was able to pray, to meet his grandfather. Every night in his closing bedtime prayer, he would ask God to bless his "Grandpa Farone" and be able to meet him one day. This was a prayer I felt would not be answered.

When my mother died, I was twelve years old, and my father grieved for a long time. Then, after ten years, he found someone and remarried. Unfortunately, his new wife wanted to start their new life together absent from my father's large family of six children and nineteen grand children. We were told not to visit anymore or even call. Basically, to disassociate ourselves from them completely. They moved two times to accomplish this goal.

Now with my father at the age of ninety years old, Nicky's new prayer was that he would get to meet his grandfather before he died. "God, I have taught Nicky all his life that nothing is impossible with You, please help," I prayed. The scripture, **"But Jesus looked at them and said to them, "With men this is impossible, but with God all things are possible," Matthew 19:26 NKJV** came to mind.

Locating my father and getting permission to see him was just the beginning. There were also the problems of transportation to take our son to see him and the money to do so. One thing at a time...

Since we went into the ministry Sandy, Nicky, and I have trusted, delighted, and committed our way to the Lord. We believed His promises. We do our best to show people that God is faithful through sacrifice. Sometimes though, God makes us wait a long time before He answers, but we have found Him always faithful.

Many times God has asked us to sacrifice our desires for the needs of others. We do it joyfully without expectation of reward.

Over the many years many people had come to work with us from various places. Some were with us for a few months and some for a year or more. We always had been able to supply them with a nice place to live, plenty of food, and all of their bills paid. God is faithful to His servants. However, not all who pledge to give to help the ministry follow through and the ministry to the children suffers. Sandy and I have agreed to put them first, no matter what the cost. So, we would make up the shortfall from our weekly salary of $300. We weren't able to save anything extra for our desires, so to make this desire of our son come true, God would have to do some big miracles.

First, we would need a good car to make the trip. Our old Ram Charger had 273,000 miles on it and now it had reached the point of fill up the oil and check the gas. It's good enough for driving around town, but not for a 3,000 mile round trip somewhere. Secondly, we had just paid the taxes for some of our workers to help them out on their tax returns, so financially we were not able to make the trip. Third, as I mentioned earlier, we didn't even know where my father lived or if my father would even want to see us. How would God answer all these needs?

Have you ever been in such a hopeless situation? Maybe you haven't seen someone you love for many years or your child has a desire you think God can't possibly answer? Maybe you think your financial situation can't change or those you trusted have let you down? Have people criticized you for your faith? We've been there. But I want you to know God is faithful.

My friend, God will not let you down if you are faithful. Man will let you down, even those who claim to be Christian will turn their back on you in a time of need, but God won't. That's why He tells us in **Colossians 3:23-24, "And whatsoever you do, do it heartily, as to the Lord and not to men, knowing that from the Lord you will receive the reward of the inheritance; for you serve the Lord Christ." NKJV**

Sitting parked in our driveway in our Ram Charger, broken down for the third time in three days, God sent a blessing to us from heaven, literally.

Those of you who have been reading my book remember the story I told about my Aunt Ginny. She and my Uncle George were such a big part of our ministry. They were the ones who provided the financing for us to purchase the Ram Charger for the ministry years before. Well, God would use them again one last time to help us in our calling.

They were not rich by any means, but had lived a comfortable life through hard work and giving. We have known few givers like them. Uncle George would say, "*Giving does the heart good.*" We learned a lot about the joy of giving from them. In the later part of the year, unexpectedly, we received a small inheritance from my aunt and uncle. It was enough to lease a good car to have for long trips, so our travel needs to see my father were met.

The following May I telephoned my sister Donna, who still lives in Schenectady. I knew if anyone in the family would know where my father lived, she would. Sure enough she did, but she said, "Dominick, I don't know if I can get through to Dad or even if you will be able to see him if I do." "Well, big sister, God can do the impossible, all we can do is try," I said. "Okay, Dom, I'll try," she said.

In faith we began to plan our trip. We had some people now we could trust to watch over the Center when we were gone. They were

The Three Dominicks

happy we were going to get away for a time of much needed refreshing. Some friends heard about us taking a trip and sent us an offering just for us. Things seemed to be coming together. Still, we had no idea we would get to see my father even if we made the long trip. He was ninety years old now, and after twenty-one years, would he even recognize me? Doubts tried to enter my mind, but I pushed ahead and did my best to ignore them. You will need to do the same in your situations as well. Don't let the devil make you doubt God.

When we got to Schenectady and went to my sister Donna's house, she was excited. "He wants to see you and meet his grandson," she said. We called him on the phone and he said, "Come on over, I'll be waiting."

As we drove up in front of the house, I saw the door swing open and my father standing there waiting. Dressed in bright red pants, blue cardigan sweater, with a scruffy white beard, and thick glasses. His smile went from ear to ear. "Hi Dad, it's Dominick, and this is Dominick Jr., your namesake," I said.

As I introduced Nicky, my Dad's eyes lit up and Nicky's eyes filled up. For the first few moments Nicky was speechless, almost as if he were holding the hand of a dream. Somehow, Nicky knew this day would come. God says we should have the faith of a child. Nicky proved it works. The desire of his heart was now a reality.

Our meeting was glorious. My Dad was shorter now, actually so am I, a little slower, and more frail, but the light in his eyes was still as bright.

As our visit ended and we pulled away I could see my father still standing in the window watching. God had given all of us our hearts desires this day.

Chapter Thirty-Six (Triumph)

"Then the Lord answered me and said: "Write the vision And make it plain on tablets, that he may run who reads it; For the vision is yet for an appointed time; But at the end it will speak, and it will not lie, Though it tarries, wait for it; Because it will surely come, It will not tarry. Behold the proud, His soul is not upright in him; But the just shall live by faith." Habakkuk 2: 2-4 NKJV

Shortly after this great miracle of seeing my Dad, I was on my knees in our sanctuary. It had nice carpet now, thanks to the Foundations, and the same altars made from a pool table we had for years. "Lord, what can I say, but thank You. Almost the entire vision You gave me five years ago has been completed. We own all the buildings and properties but the one building, the State Motor Vehicle Building, and that's okay, I am so thankful." Then I heard a familiar voice say to me, "You stopped walking."

I didn't move. I kept my eyes closed. I changed the subject. "Lord, I really enjoy the Youth Ensemble You gave us and the bus You provided to travel in."

Sandy and I decided we would do something special for the kids who were growing. The ones who were working hard to follow the

Lord and who showed up every week for service. This would be an incentive to the other kids. We created our first Youth Ensemble. We had our mission bus painted and our pastor friends around the country invited us to come and do special services at their churches. Those adventures alone would fill another book.

As I mentioned earlier in the book, we had a Camp-mobile made from an old bread truck that someone donated so we could take our Youth camping on the weekends to the State Park that was close by. We had all we needed.

White Bus

Camp Mobile

But the vision wasn't complete without the one last building to complete it. The State Motor Vehicle building I saw as a school of some kind. "That's okay, God, that's okay, I am so grateful," I said. When God gives you a vision, it's not complete until He says it's complete. God won't give you less than He promises, unless you stop believing He will.

All my efforts to distract God had failed and He said again, "You stopped walking."

Slowly I rose from my knees. Slowly I exited the sanctuary door. And as slowly as possible, I began to walk towards the last building, the State Motor Vehicle building. It also had two parking lots with the property. Approaching the building, I noticed something strange. There were no cars parked there. There were no people milling around. Walking closer, there was a tiny slip of paper taped to the front door. It read, "*Have moved to new location*." I froze in my tracks.

"What?" I said. I couldn't believe my eyes. What should I do? I walked around it eight times and claimed it as an Education building for the kids, as it appeared in my vision.

Going back to my office I called the Governor right away to tell him about the note. "Dave, you won't believe what I just saw. The building next to us is closed and they have moved." I said. "Yes I know," he said. "I'm working on it right now to see if I can get a lease on it for you for $1.00 a year for the next thirty years. They are going to auction the building off in a month for $60,000.00. It's valued at $88,000.00 so it would be a good deal, but there's no way I can find the money in that short amount of time. Let me see if I can get them to lease it to you, I'll get back in touch," he said and hung up.

"Well, God, it's in your hands. There's nothing I can do. If it's Your will, Dave will come through, if not that's okay, I am most grateful for all You have given us," I said.

Two weeks had passed and no word from Dave. I kept myself busy building things, fixing things, working with the Youth, doing services, running the restaurant three nights a week, and I had a full plate, as they say. (No pun intended.)

We had learned, as a family over the years, to keep our priorities straight. It is God first, family second, and ministry third. We would not let the ministry take over. We had seen too many pastors lose their families when they put the ministry first and their families in second place. We kept Mondays as a family day. We would go to a movie and dinner or a park or something, just no ministry work on that day.

Now it was Tuesday, and I arrived early at my office to get things ready for the day. Someone else arrived early that day too. "Good morning, Nick." It was Clarke. "I wanted to see how you are doing and if you had any needs?" he said. This could not be a coincidence; there are no coincidences with God.

He had done so much already I didn't want him to think I was greedy. "We're doing fine," I said. "However, there is this one thing that just popped up," I said. "What is it?" He was very interested. "Well, the office building over there (pointing to the building), is going to be auctioned off in two weeks, and I have always seen it as an Education Building. A place we could teach kids, like a school," I said. "Will you make it a school?" Clarke said. "Yes sir, that's how I saw it in my vision almost five years ago," I said. "How much do they want?" he asked. "Well, they are going to start the bidding at $60,000.00, so I don't know. It's worth $88,000.00 as it is now," I said. "I'll have a check to you by the end of the week and don't you waiver," he said pointing his finger at me to affirm what he said. Sure enough, by Friday I had a check for $65,000.00 from Clarke.

Two weeks later one of my directors and I were standing on the street corner by the office building waiting for the auction. There was another man there who looked terribly eager. As the auction started I had no idea what to do, so I ask my friend who was with me. He said he would help. "Okay, who will give $60,000.00 for this building," the auctioneer said. My friend said, "Raise your hand," so I did. "Okay, who will give $61,000.00," the auctioneer bellowed. I raised my hand again quickly. "No, you don't bid against yourself," the auctioneer said. So I put my hand down. I was so eager my first time out of the gate.

Although there was only one other person there, he was just as eager. Then a weird thing happened. It appeared that he was trying to talk and make a bid, but someone or something was holding his lips closed. He sort of hummed loudly shaking his head. Not being able to get a word out the auctioneer said, "Sold for 60,000.00 to New Beginnings." I couldn't believe it. The building and both parking lots were now ours. We could make it a learning center for the kids, just like in my vision.

I went right to my office and called Clarke to tell him the good news. "Thank you so much, I'll send the extra $5,000.00 back to you right away," I said. "No need, you keep it for something for the Center," he said and hung up.

Those two parking lots were being used on the weekends by drug dealers, in the middle of the night, to do their dealings. So we used the extra $5,000.00 to put up a nine foot, nine gage, chain link fence around the property. No more drug dealing in that neighborhood.

Chapter Thirty-Seven (Triumph)

"But as for me, I trust in You, O Lord; I say, "You are my God." My times are in Your hand." Psalm 31:14-15 NKJV

We had all the properties and buildings I saw in my vision, but it was not yet complete. I have a saying, "*God moves fast, God moves slow, when He moves fast, you have to be ready to go.*" I was ready, but God wasn't. I have learned it is always better to wait on the Lord and to trust Him.

We continued to work on and started using the restaurant. I still wondered what we could do with the empty lot next to it. I saw kids playing in it when I had my vision.

What would bring the kids and community support to this spot? What would benefit the restaurant? A Putt Putt Golf Course! There wasn't a miniature golf course within a hundred miles at that time. But could I get one that would fit on such a small lot?

In contacting a number of miniature golf companies in the country, we found one that said every restaurant they put one at increased their business income. I mentioned the small area we had and they said to just send them the dimensions. They would design something just for us. They also said they would give us a $20,000.00 discount on the price, as a donation to the work we were doing with the children.

After a few days, they got back to me with a quote for $65,000.00. That number rang a bell. That was the exact amount I had just invested in the Education Building that was worth $88,000.00. Hmmm! Off to the bank I went and the bank President said, "No problem." They would give me the money and hold our Education building as collateral.

In two months I finally saw clearly what I couldn't make out at first in my vision. Now you get to see it complete.

Our business doubled as soon as it was opened.

Vacant Lot

Putt Putt Golf Course

Chapter Thirty-Eight (Trial)

"Train up a child the way he should go, and when he is old, he will not depart from it." Proverbs 22:6 NKJV

I had my hands full with running the restaurant, youth center, services on Sunday, and traveling to raise funds. Sandy started "Tea with Jesus" classes that taught our girls to appreciate who they were as young ladies, as well as running the Christian Shop. She taught our girls personal hygiene, manners, and etiquette. Those with perfect attendance were rewarded with a special night out. We took the girls for a dinner at a fine restaurant to test their training. I got to go because I drove them in our van.

We contacted one of the restaurants in a larger city close by and told them our plan. We asked them to set their tables five-star restaurant fashion for us. The girls were all excited and never felt so special in all their young lives. We even bought our girls nice dresses to wear and keep to remember their special night. It's so funny! I remember one of our girls was afraid to eat the cherries jubilee the chef prepared special for them, because he lit it on fire. Her eyes couldn't get any bigger watching him put her dessert up in flames. After some reassurance, by Sandy, that it was okay, she tasted it and sheer delight came over her face. Then she wouldn't let anybody else have a taste, it was all hers.

You may think this was just something that was fun for them, but let me tell you how it changed one young lady's life in particular.

One day a young girl came to our Center. She was thirteen years old. She dressed like a man, never smiled, and was tough as nails. She didn't like men and bonded to Sandy quickly. Sandy has that way about her. That's her gift from God. It takes time to change a life, as I have mentioned before, and Sandy would invest that time. She would come when Sandy was supervising the Youth Center after school and help her out. She eventually became one of our Youth Leaders. She was as tough as any of the boys so when we had a problem, we would send her to "speak" to the problem maker. They knew she meant business and ended their disputes quickly.

Getting to know her we discovered this young girl had been physically abused by every man her mother knew. There was no father in the home. She was given to men in exchange for drugs or alcohol since she was eleven years old. Now I understood why she dressed like a man.

Little by little, as she got to know us, she felt respected and appreciated for the first time in her life. Sandy and I had entered into a dark part of life most people don't even know about, much less live. "God, help us reach these kids for You and let them know they are loved just as they are and loved for who they are," Sandy and I prayed daily.

One day I got a call from the counselor at the Middle School. "I'd like to speak to Pastor Farone," the person said. "This is he how can I help you?" I said. "I need to have you come into my office regarding one of the girls that comes to your Center," he said. "Who are we talking about?" I asked. It was this child that had been raped most of her life and we were now hoping to reach for our Lord. "Okay, I'll be right there," I said.

I didn't know what to expect. I felt the devil may have them thinking I was abusing this girl. Rumors had been used before by the devil to ruin many works and people. All you have to do is say something and people believe the worst.

One time we had an older couple working with us and the children really bonded to the senior gentleman. He became sort of a grandfather figure, they called him "Pa Pa." One of the "non-resident" fathers felt their son was growing too attached to him, so he spread the word that he was a child molester. Even though that was totally false, it ended the ministry and reputation of this sweet man and the couple left the city.

When I arrived at the counselor's office I was escorted in and the door was shut behind me. "Reverend Farone, have a seat," he said. 'The reason you are here is there are some questions I need answered. We have seen quite a change in one of our girls here. She comes to your Center. Her name is so-and-so, and there has been quite a change in her over these last few months. She has changed her appearance to dress a little more feminine. She is also doing better in her classes. She is not as hostile to her teachers as she was. I had her come into my office and asked her what was causing her to make these positive changes. The first thing she said was she was attending church regularly and loved the Center. She said she helps Miss Sandy out there during the week." "Yes, all that is true," I said. "Sandy is my wife and she has great love for the girls. Some of them even call her 'Mama Sandy,'" I said.

"Well, apparently she also thinks very highly of you," he said. "As we were talking she said there is only one man she trusts in her life, and that's Pastor Nick. I wanted to thank you personally and to tell you that whatever you are doing there, to keep it up. You are changing the lives of these young people." Then he shook my hand and I left his office humbled and relieved. What a blessing this precious child of God brought into our lives.

In February of 2005 Sandy received wonderful recognition for her work with the Youth in the city. God always honors those who honor Him. She was awarded the Nathan Bolton Award for community service.

Outside entrance to Sandy's Christian Shop

Inside Christian Shop

Sandy at her desk

Chapter Thirty-Nine (Trial)

"So I will restore to you the years that the swarming locust has eaten....You shall eat in plenty and be satisfied, And praise the name of the Lord your God, Who has dealt wondrously with you; And My people shall never be put to shame." Joel 25, 26 NKJV

It was early in the morning on August 29, 2005. A Category 3 hurricane called "Katrina" struck the Gulf Coast of the United States. With sustained winds of 100-140 miles an hour, it devastated homes, businesses, and lives. Its torrential rains and winds damaged some of our roofs at the Center and did a lot of water damage in our buildings. We were basically shut down from the damage. It would take time and *a lot of money* to restore all, but we still had the Youth Mission House that was usable.

Many people were displaced by the storm, and we wanted to do what we could to help. We received a call from a couple who said they had two children and lost their home in the storm, down in south Louisiana. They asked if we had a place they could stay until they got back on their feet. The quickest way to have your needs met is to help with the needs of others. Our Youth House was available so I said, "Come on up."

Pulling into our parking lot in a van loaded with everything you could imagine, they arrived. "Welcome, I'm Pastor Nick and we want to help you through this hard time," I said. Our Youth House was completely furnished so all they had to do was move in, and they did.

A few weeks passed and the gentleman would leave every day and do carpentry work back in their old home area. The lady and her two children, who were teenagers, would stay and help hand out food and clothing at places the city had set up for Katrina victims. This was the regular routine until one cold day in October.

"Pastor Nick, your place is on fire," I got a call from the local Sheriff. Rushing over to the Youth House, I saw the family standing outside while the firemen smashed out the upstairs bedroom windows. "What happened?" I asked the couple. "A candle I had lit in the bedroom fell over and caught the curtains on fire," the woman said. "Are you all okay?" I asked. "Yes, we are fine, we made it out with our dog before the firemen got here," the man said.

Having put the fire out, the Fire Chief came over to me and said, "You were lucky, Pastor Nick. Somehow the fire stayed contained to that one bedroom and we were able to put it out quickly." "Thank you," I said.

That night we put the couple and their children up at a hotel and started making plans on what to do. We had no insurance on the building so we were in trouble. Now the whole Center would be shut down and take years to restore.

The folks we had taken in were taken care of at the hotel. Their room and food were paid for by Katrina funds, but there was no help for us.

A month later they moved back to their home down south and had taken most of the things we had provided for them to use. TV, stereos, kitchen appliances, all the things we had in our Youth House. We just gave it up to God.

There I sat in my wet office, all alone. The place shut down from the storms, house burned, and needing $14,000.00 to repair just the house from the fire. There was no hope in sight. I'd have to go on the road again to raise the funds, but I felt defeated. Just the house alone would take many churches to visit. "God, I'm all out of faith," I said. "If this work is done, it's done. I don't see how we can keep going."

God knows when your spirit is broken and He will do the unexpected to let you know He is still in control.

Chapter Forty (Triumph)

"Delight yourself also in the Lord and He shall give you the desires of your heart." Psalm 37:4

One of the "Bucket List" things Sandy and I wanted to do in our lives was to go to Hawaii. Once we went into the ministry and decided to give most of the money we received away, it made that desire now totally impossible. Yet God does say, **"Delight yourself also in the Lord and He shall give you the desires of your heart." Psalm 37:4** Nothing about a "Bucket List." I like God's word better.

In January 2006 some people wanted to give us a break from all the battles we were facing and God provided a "Cruise to Hawaii." A first class cruise with a mini suite. He does bless those who serve Him when they are "not" serving Him with their own desires as their goal.

We felt our ministry was over and God was giving us a farewell blessing. As we were waiting to board the ship, I commented to Sandy, "Look at all these old people." They say the longer the cruise, the older the people. Probably because at that time in your life you have saved enough to take one. That is also why what happened next was so strange. I heard someone laugh. "I know that voice," I said to Sandy. "There it is again, doesn't that sound like Ken?" I said. "Yes," she said. "And that sounds like Cheri," Sandy said. Lo and behold it was our dear friends we hadn't seen in a while. Ken was one of my original Board Members and Cheri was one of Sandy's good friends. They were taking the cruise with Cheri's family and had no idea we would be taking the cruise. God always has a plan. After telling them about what had happened at the Center, Ken scheduled me right away to do a service at his church. God's miracles didn't stop there. Sandy and I did all the "Touristy" things in Hawaii. Walked in a dormant volcano, went to the rainforest, ate at a luau, etc. It was our dream come true! God was also restoring the dream He had for us and our ministry.

When you take a cruise many times you are assigned to a particular table to eat dinner. You get to know the folks you are dining with pretty well. Dot and Les were two such folks, and we became lifelong friends. Before leaving the ship that day, returning to Los Angeles, they gave the ministry a check for $1,000.00 to help it get back on its feet. They have remained faithful supporters, through thick and thin, ever since. This was just the beginning...

Chapter Forty-One (Triumph)

"He shall pray to God, and He will delight in Him. He shall see His face with joy, for He restores to man His righteousness." Job 33:26 NKJV

Returning home after our "Miracle Cruise" I realized if we had to go back on the road, full-time, to restore the Center, we would need another RV to live and travel in. We had no money in the bank so again we felt there was no way. We could go to the churches in the South for services, but California was out of the question. The idea came to Sandy that it would take a miracle of God.

Sitting in a Cracker Barrel restaurant, after doing a service in south Mississippi, I said to Sandy, "We have the tour bus we can't use anymore. It has a diesel gas engine and at $4.00 a gal, getting four miles a gallon, and having a 176-gallon tank, its days were over for traveling. Why don't we see if someplace will take our tour bus as a trade in for an RV we can travel and live in?" "Sounds crazy," Sandy said. But the idea was persistent.

I took a napkin and drew a picture of the exact layout we wanted in the RV and stuck it in my pocket. Driving home from the restaurant, in the rain, we were about to pass an RV sales place. I turned to look at Sandy and said, "Why not?"

Pulling into the RV sales store a man came running out to meet us. "Come in out of the rain," he said and ushered us into his office. "What can I do for you?" he asked. "Well sir, we are looking to buy a new RV to travel in for ministry. I have a picture I drew of the layout we want and if you have one we will buy it right now," I said with such confidence. Pulling out the napkin in my pocket and handing it to him, we sat down. Taking a few seconds to look at it he said, "I'll be right back," and left the room.

He came back shortly and said, "Yes, we have one exactly like this. Do you have something you would like to trade in?" "Yes, we do. We have a tour bus that is in great shape, freshly painted, and has forty-six seats. I have a picture of it to show you in our ministry booklet, if you'd like to see it, and I can have the bus here tomorrow," I said. I ran out to the car to get the booklet I had put together of the ministry progress since 1994 called, "God's Vision Coming to Fruition." He looked at it and said, "I'll be right back" and left the room.

He was gone for quite a while this time, so I thought like Sandy did, "Sounds crazy."

About twenty minutes had passed and he came back. "If your bus is in as good a shape as you say, we have a deal," he said. We shook hands on it and Sandy and I left.

The next day, Monday, I drove our tour bus to the RV dealership and drove home with a brand new "Class C" RV to travel to California in for ministry the next month.

But God didn't stop there.

While we were in California I received a phone call, "Is this Rev. Nick Farone?" the caller inquired. "Yes it is, who is this?" I said. "You don't know me, but we just bought your bus," he said. "We have a ministry in Gautier, MS, and we were driving down the road and saw your bus sitting at the RV Dealership. It already had our name on it, so we felt like it was meant for us. Our ministry is called New Beginnings," he said. "That is amazing!" I said. "Even more so because our ministry started in the south at a small church in Gautier, MS, eighteen years ago," I said. We both laughed at the timing of God's plan for both of us.

Isn't God so Amazing?

Chapter Forty-Two (Triumph)

"Now to Him who is able to do exceedingly, abundantly above all that we ask or think, according to the power that works in us." Ephesians 3:20 NKJV

After doing services for Ken, we reunited with other dear friends in California, Pete and Linda, who invited us to their church to help. Then we returned home.

It was June of 2006, and I had a dream. I was calling a man I once saw do a Bible teaching using large charts on the Christian TV Station in Monroe, LA. God was telling me to do a revival at his church, but to do it backwards. God said to do it in July when most pastors don't schedule revivals and doing it backwards means starting on a Wednesday night and finishing up on a Sunday morning. Most revivals start on a Sunday morning and finish up on a Wednesday night. I called the pastor and told him what I believed God told me to do. He was a little cautious never having me at his church before so he said, "I'll pray about it." Well, I told you earlier what that usually means, so I just thought I must have missed it.

Not long after my call, he called me back. "Okay, I can't tell you who or how many will be here in the month of July, but if you will come and take whatever the offering is, you are welcomed to come," he said. "I'll be there," I said.

Arriving in Norfolk, VA, I didn't know it was the home of a large military base. The pastor was so gracious and welcomed us with open arms. That Wednesday night we had a pretty good crowd. I usually give my testimony at the first service, but God told me to do that last. I ministered in the order of the services God arranged for me. Services were being blessed and growing every night in attendance. The church was having a men's breakfast that Saturday morning. The pastor asked me to sing a couple of songs and speak for about fifteen minutes about our work. There would be about fifteen men with their wives at this breakfast.

At 8:00 A.M. I was setting up my sound system in the small room that sat about thirty people around tables, where we could have something to eat together. "Lord, I have no idea what to sing or say this morning, please guide me," I prayed.

"Sing something patriotic," came His familiar voice from within. "That's a great idea," I said out loud. Good thing I was alone. Breakfast was over and now it was my time to minister. I sang a couple of songs and all of the men stood to their feet. It was a wonderful patriotic moment we all shared. We all sat down, and I briefly told them why I was on the road and that we needed $14,000.00 to restore our Youth House. I told them I would not go back home until I reached my goal, then I sat down.

After I finished the pastor stood up to close out the breakfast with a prayer. He was a very dignified man, not prone to emotion, from what I saw over the past few days. Yet, when he went to speak, he began to cry. Composing himself, he tried again. Same thing happened. He couldn't speak. Now, I was starting to tear up myself. What was happening? The other men and women also began to tear up.

Finally, he said, "This is not right that these children do not have their home, we need to take care of this. My wife and I are taking $1,000.00 out of our savings to give Pastor Nick, and I know some of you can do the same. I know some of you can give $5,000 and it wouldn't hurt you. We need to meet this need. I'm going to pass the hat right now and see what we come up with." Then he proceeded to pass a hat.

"Eleven thousand dollars, that's good. Thank you. We will meet the rest of this need on Sunday in the offering," the Pastor said. My emotions gripped me, and I couldn't leave the room for quite a while. I know I'm a cry baby, but this was God all the way.

After service that Sunday Pastor handed me a check and said, "We met your need and gave you a little extra. We wanted to be part of your wonderful work. God Bless You." We hugged, and I opened the check. It was for $18,000.00!

What more can I say to prove God is faithful when we are?

Repaired Mission House

We celebrated by painting our Youth Center in bright rainbow colors to show we were back, better than ever, and God was restoring.

Two years later God had restored all, and we were back in the front pages again.

Chapter Forty-Three (Triumph)

"...for he who honors me, I will honor." 1 Samuel 2:30 NKJV

"Faith and Values"

The News - Star Saturday April 5, 2008

At New Beginnings the Rev. Nick Farone introduces youth to a healthy lifestyle through diet, recreation, and worship. On any given Tuesday through Saturday, the youth recreation center is a hub of foosh-ball, pool, and other activities and games for children and through it, the Rev. Nick Farone has tried to teach kids more than just how to shoot pool. In the 14 years of its existence New Beginnings Christian Youth Center has been a recreation center, a place of learning, a house of worship, and a training center for thousands of children. "The parents feel good about leaving their kids here because they know they're supervised," Farone said. "They won't get into trouble." The ministry began in 1994, and has evolved over the years, with New Beginnings holding Children worship services and hosting classes to teach children about etiquette and health issues. Also opened for a time were The Blessing Restaurant and a Christian Store. Both served as training facilities for the youth to learn about working. "The best way to teach our kids is to show them," Farone said.

Farone has been able to take kids on sponsored mission trips to see another country, he said. "For seven years, I would take the kids to Mexico," Farone said. "We would go and minister to kids who had nothing and it was such a witness to my kids here." Farone said he and his wife Sandy also put together a youth ensemble with requirements that participants have good grades in school, a good attitude, and enjoy singing. "All of those things, if they did them, we took them around the country," he said. "They got recognized in places like Japan and Israel because they got written up in a magazine."

In recent years, Farone began a program called, "Recapturing Healthy Lifestyles for Our Youth," "This aim is to teach children about eating healthy and exercise," he said. "We found out if we get them eating right and exercising, it improves their grades, it improves their mental capacity, it improves their social skills," Farone said. "For example, they would learn how to eat a healthy breakfast, they would learn to get away from sodas and candies and replace that with fruit and vegetables. They tried it and they learned they felt so much better, and they got excited."

Following the success of the program, Farone said the ministry is in the process of applying for a grant. "If we get the funding, we'll be able to reach 160 kids a day, as opposed to, we're up to 30," he said. "I think the government sees the need for it, and I think we've proven ourselves over the last 15 years that we have real credibility."

Chapter Forty-Four (Triumph)

"For all the promises of God in Him are Yes, and in Him Amen, to the glory of God through us." 2 Corinthians 1:2 NKJV

There was no doubt in my life now, after living totally by faith, with my family, that all of God's promises are true. It was time for me to complete the promise I had made to Him on 8-8-1988.

It was *August 2008*. Through much hard work and travel God had restored much of the Center again. We couldn't open the restaurant or Christian shop yet because we had to travel to keep the funds coming in and had no time to oversee these outreaches as we did before. All in God's time we learned. We had reached an income of $165,000.00 in donations, our credit was A plus rating, and my time to fulfill the vow I made twenty years ago had arrived.

I was now an Ordained Bishop with the Church of God in Cleveland, TN, and was invited to attend their General Council in San Antonio, TX, that summer. I even had my own table display in the main room to promote New Beginnings and the work we were doing with God's Youth. I remember it was a HUGE! room with massive, costly displays all around for various ministry outreaches. I felt really out of place being there with my small eight-by-four-foot table of fliers and a video we had showing the center and us winning the Angel Award grant. We took one of our Youth with us to sit at the table, when we couldn't be there, to push the button and re-start the video every three and a half minutes. Taking a break from the Convention activities and walking around the room looking at the many displays, I came across Pathway Books/Derek Press.

Stopping by their table a man named Mike came up to me."Are you looking to have your book published?" he said. "You've got to be kidding me!" I said. "I do have a book. I have been writing it for twenty years and this is the exact month I needed to find a publisher. I am here promoting our work with the Youth in Louisiana and just happened to be walking around."

"Well, tell me a little about yourself and your book and we will see what we can do," he said. After talking for about thirty minutes he said, "We'd like to publish your book." I said, "Well, I'd need someone to put it all together for me, lay it out, do whatever book publishers do, and tell me what I need to pay for." "You just send me what you have and we will work to give you the book you want," he said. AND...that's how ***Faith How It Works*** got done. Twenty years to the day from when I made my promise.

Cover of my first book

Chapter Forty-Five (Trial)

"He shall bring forth your righteousness as the light, And your justice as the noonday." Psalm 37: 6 NKJV

The same month God fulfilled the vow I made to Him, to publish a book about His faithfulness for twenty years, the devil unleashed his greatest attack against us. There is no doubt that the devil hates those God uses to do His work. It was so blatantly evident in this attack.

Over the years the city's—I emphasize *THE CITY'S*—storm drain under one of our parking lots would cave in. The cement piping it flowed through was there from the 1920s and was now giving way to age. Two times over the past two years, when it did so, I would simply call the Mayor and he would send over his work crew and have it fixed within days. However, this time the hole was massive and the Mayor simply refused my calls. I wrote letters, but they were ignored as well. I spoke to one of my friends in the city. He was a judge there for many years until he retired. He said, "Nick, the city knows it's their drain and their problem. They have been fixing it for years. Just get a lawyer to send them a letter and they will get to it in no time." So that's what we did. The city decided to have me take them to court and thought because as a minister I had no money, I would just let it drop. The hole got bigger and bigger. It became known as the city "Crater."

A year passed and the city judge finally set a court date. It would be another six months just to hear our case. I was ready. I had documents, photos, depositions from city workers, and from the caretakers that were living on the property at that time. No way could we lose.

I was invited to go to Italy and Germany to minister in music and the Word by the director of the Ministry to the Military with the Church of God. What a blessing this was, and it gave me two weeks before the trial to get back home.

I had no sooner got to Germany and I received a call from Sandy, who was holding down the fort for us while I was ministering. "Nick, we just got a letter from our lawyer saying he is quitting, he is just too busy, and wants to be paid." "What???" I was in shock and now I only had two weeks to find another lawyer, pay our lawyer, and have all the documentation transferred to a new lawyer, and I WAS IN GERMANY!!! What to do? What to do? "Relax and trust Me," I heard an inner voice say. Then I remembered a man I met years ago at the Christian TV Station that said he was a lawyer. I told Sandy to call him and see if he would take the case. He said yes, if I would pay him upfront so much money. I told Sandy to give him what we had and I would pay him the rest from my services when I got home. He said okay. Soon I found out that our first lawyer had a chance to become the city attorney.

Coincidence? I don't think so.

So we made it to court on time, with a new lawyer. As I entered the courtroom I noticed the judge talking to our Mayor. "Ut, oh! That's not good," I thought.

"No matter, I have so much evidence, so many photos and witnesses, I can't lose," I thought.

As the proceedings started our lawyer stood up and said, "Your Honor, I'd like to call my first witness." As I began to get up the city's attorney said, "Your honor I would like to have this witness be disqualified because he was not placed on the witness list."My lawyer jumped up and said, "But your honor it is his ministry bringing the suit. There was no need to put him on the witness list." The judge simply looked over at me and said, "Witness disqualified. Next witness."

Long story short, within fifteen minutes the judge decided in the city's favor and he and the Mayor went out to lunch.

However, there was another lawyer in the courtroom that day. He was a friend of our lawyer who was just defeated on behalf of the city. He said to our lawyer, "This is just not right. If Nick will let me sign the agreement with you, I will file for appeal, pay the court costs myself, and fight this for him." And so it was...

The city would get the judges to put off our court dates. Mayors changed, the judges changed, and city attorneys stayed the same. We lost most of our Foundations support because we had to keep the Center closed and safe for the children. The "Crater" grew across our parking lot and even to the basketball court. Sandy and I sacrificed our home and personal things to keep what bills we could paid. The city just sat and watched.

Chapter Forty-Six (Trial)

"Beloved, you do faithfully whatever you do for the brethren and for strangers, who have borne witness of your love before the church. If you send them forward on their journey in a manner worthy of God, you will do well." 3 John 1: 5-6 NKJV

In the summer of 2010, as we waited for the next court date in our fight against the city, we continued to minister in churches around the country. We had just left a church on the road in Michigan/Indiana, just on the border. The folks there call it "Michiana." While we were there terrible storms hit and a tree limb smashed our windshield on the RV, but it was still okay to see through. We were heading out to see Nicky at ORU for a brief visit before returning home.

In a place called Bartlett, Kansas, the thermostat started to rise on the engine in the RV. It started to overheat and within minutes, before I could stop and check it out, it blew! All the lights on the dashboard began flashing and we were stranded just outside the town. We had RV insurance to tow us to the nearest gas station, but where was it? I barely had cell phone reception, but I finally reached somebody. "Well sir, ya see, we will have to send a tow truck from Joplin, Missouri, because that's the closet we can find from where you are at," the fella said. "Bartlett's a very small town and there's not much there, it'll take some time so just sit tight," he said and hung up. Where's was I gonna go? I thought.

Three hours later a huge tow truck showed up and towed us ten miles into the town that had two stop lights, one at the beginning of the town and one at the end. The town had one grocery store and kitty corner from that was the town bar. One gas station and outside of town one auto repair shop. I asked the tow truck guy to stop so I could ask at the corner store if anyone in town worked on RVs. I went inside the grocery store and spoke to the lady behind the counter. "Yes sir, there's a fella just on the other side of town that works on big vehicles," she said. So I had the tow guy deposit us there right in front of a big garage, thanked him, and we said our farewells.

Early next morning a young man, I'd say in his late thirties, arrived and was looking over our RV. "Good morning," I said. "I hear you work on RVs?" "Yes sir, I do. What seems to be the problem, other than your busted windshield?" he said. He had already noticed the black oil all over the front of the RV. "I don't know, all of a sudden it just overheated and died," I said. "It sure did," he said. "That motor is gone you're gonna need a new one." "A New One?" I said. "Yes, I'm sorry but there is nothing I can do with that, it is totally frozen up and damaged. I can tell just by the way your front is all covered with oil. I'll check it out and see, but I'm pretty sure I'm right," he said.

The next day he did just that, and he was right. It was gone. "Now what do we do?" I asked. "Well, just leave your RV here, I called the factory and they can ship a new one out next week and I can get started pulling the old one out in the meantime. The motor alone will cost $4,500.00. I can replace the windshield for you while I'm working and the insurance will pay for that, but your RV warranty is over so, with my labor cost, it will be $7,000.00." My eyes sort of glazed over and I thought, "There's no way I can come up with that money. We barely get by with the ministry bills we pay now, since we lost most of our Foundation monies. We are done." I didn't know what to say, what to do, or where to go. Ever been there?

Just then my cell phone rang, which was a miracle in itself because we got very little reception. It was one of my Board members and closest friends. "I was just praying for you and God impressed on me to give you a call," he said. "Are you okay?" he asked. I can't believe this, I thought to myself. This was the one man who could help us, but I would have never asked. He and his wife were dear friends from the beginning of our ministry on the road, and this was truly a "God thing."

I told them our story and he said, "We will have to move some money around but tell the fellow we will send the money next week. You can pay me back when you get it," he said. I was overjoyed and said, "Don't worry about your loan, just consider it money in God's bank and no matter how long it takes, I will pay it back with interest."

Two months later the RV was fixed and back home in our driveway ready for our next ministry trip to California in February of 2011.

Chapter Forty-Seven (Trial)

"Yet, in all these things we are more than conquerors through Him who loved us." Romans 8:37 NKJV

It was now February 4, 2011, and the city had once again put our trial date off another year. I had faced bureaucracy many times fighting for the children over the years, but never like this. Nothing I could do but leave it in our lawyer's hands that I believe God provided. So off we were headed for a month of ministry in California with some of our favorite churches and friends to raise funds for the ministry.

We were on our favorite road, interstate I-10, looking forward to our trip. People used to ask Nicky where he grew up and he'd say, "Interstate 10." They'd laugh, but he wasn't joking. Sandy was driving behind me in our car. We felt spending a month in California it was cheaper than renting one.

A few hours out horror struck! I saw the needle on the thermostat start rising the same way it did, just before the motor blew. I quickly pulled over and called the fellow who had just installed the new motor. "Hello, my name is... prepare to die!" No I didn't use the line from *Princess Bride*, but I thought about it. "Hello, this is Rev. Nick Farone," before I could continue our mechanic said, "Hi, how are you, is everything all right?" "Well, no, the RV motor is doing exactly what it did just before it blew last time," I said. "Okay, do me a favor, just go out, open the hood, and hold the radiator hose, see if it is hot," he said.

Following his instructions I did as he said. "Okay, it's not hot, so now what?" I said. "Well, you can do two things. Drive it under twenty-five miles an hour and bring it back here, or take it to the nearest major Ford Dealer and have them check it out. It could be a faulty thermostat or the witchit, googly gook, flowstruct, cummerbun, inside the motor." Those last words were mine as I have no idea what he was talking about. "Well, it's too far to bring it back. If it blows up again on the road I will just have to leave it where it dies. The next major Ford dealership is 300 miles from where I am now, so I guess I'll just try and get it there," I said. "Good luck," he said and we hung up.

So there we were going twenty-five miles an hour on Interstate 10. Me with the RV flashers on, and Sandy behind me following with the car flashers on. I have a great wife! I have never heard so many car horns or seen so many hand gestures in all my life. We would drive and when the RV went over twenty-five miles an hour it would overheat again. I'd pull over until it cooled off.

After four hours of this we had only gone 100 miles of the 300 needed to reach the Ford Dealership. I was determined not to leave the RV along the roadside somewhere. Then I began to notice something. When we went downhill I could reach forty-five miles an hour, but as we began to climb the RV would get over heated. God gave me an idea. When we would go downhill I put the RV in neutral, turned off the engine, and coasted. When we started going uphill again, I would start the RV and drive until we came to another hill. I would repeat the process again and again. "Hey, this is great! No more hand gestures," I told Sandy on the cell phone. I even reached fifty-five miles an hour sometimes going downhill with no overheating.

As we approached El Paso, TX, I was inspired. "Sandy, let's not stop in El Paso. Let's just keep going to that campground we like in Tucson, AZ. We can park at the RV park there, do services in California from there with our car, and take the RV to the big Ford dealership on Monday," I said. She agreed.

That Monday I took it to the Dealership, and they did a $350.00 diagnostic and said, "It may be the thermostat or it could be a faulty witchit, googly gook, flowstruct, cummerbun, inside the motor. We'd have to take the motor apart that would cost around $3,500.00."

So back to the campground God had brought us to. There we would stay until we won our court case and receive the monies lost. Then we would have the money to find out about the faulty witchit, googly gook, flowstruct, cummerbun, inside the motor.

Actually it ended up being just me with faithful Shakespeare staying in the RV. Sandy had to go back to Louisiana to take care of her mother and oversee the Center. God provided in various ways for Sandy to come and visit me and Shakespeare every six months.

"Never give up! Never Surrender!" A quote from the movie *Galaxy Quest* is true.

Years passed, and in November of 2014 we decided not to reopen the Center again and wait for God to send the right person to take it over and to the next level. Sandy's mom had reached a point where she could no longer live alone. She would need Sandy to be with her 24/7.

I didn't know it at the time, but one day I heard that the campground I had been staying at for the past three years and nine months in the RV also had places you could rent on a yearly basis. With only two weeks to prepare, they had a place ready and waiting for us all to live together. Now Sandy's mom could have the care she needed.

Chapter Forty-Eight (Triumph)

"He shall bring forth your righteousness as the light and your justice as the noonday." Psalm 37:6 NKJV

Our lawyers went to the Supreme Court twice over the many years. The city appealed the first time, but when they voted unanimously again the second time in our favor, it was done and evident that we were right.

We won our case for the last time on September 29, 2015. Our lawyers got paid, we received a settlement to fix the hole, and we could now fill the storm drain with rocks like we wanted to eight years hence. Actually, we received so little from the long battle our part of the settlement wouldn't even pay for the rocks, but we did win.

Sandy and I lost much in the battle, but when you are fighting for justice and truth, you must continue. God said He will bring forth our righteousness as the light and our justice as the noonday. And He did!

We have always known this mighty work would continue and to do so it would have to be taken over by the right man and woman. A man and woman who had the same heart and calling as God had placed on Sandy and I. No, it would not be our son, Dominick Jr., as most people would expect. God had His own plans prepared for him and Jacqui. In a city that is seventy-eight percent African American, we felt God would send someone of that race who would not have to fight the prejudice we faced the entire twenty years we were there. God had given us great favor with the kids, despite our skin color. We taught them from the beginning that God does not look at the outside, but at the inside. He sees our hearts. And we are right...

In November of 2015 there was a Bishop from another denomination traveling through our city on his way to minister in Arkansas. After dining at the local corner restaurant downtown, just off the square, he decided to take a walk around the corner and exercise his morning meal. As he did, he noticed our main building with the plaque on the front door that read, "*Founded by Rev. Nick, Sandy, and Dominick Farone Jr. July 1996.*" The center was shut down, and looking around he could see it was once a mighty work. At that moment God spoke to him and said, "I want you to restore this work in honor of the man who founded it to the glory of God." The Bishop knew the voice of the Lord and shared this experience with his wife. Right away he went about trying to make contact with me through our realtor friend, Marla. Getting in touch with Marla, he made an offer that would have paid off most of the ministry debts we still had left from the seven-year battle with the city.

Months went by and we heard nothing. We found out that the bank would not allow the loan for his offer, even though it was half of what the ministry was worth. More months went by and God kept our ministry on his heart. Passing through the city in June of 2016, Marla decided to give him a call. Getting in touch with him she said, "Make an offer." He did, and when Marla called me I felt a nudge in my heart to agree. Even though it would leave the ministry owing a great deal, I felt God would one day pay off the debt.

The most important thing was to get the ministry back open for the children. It is His work and I was just the steward He trusted to establish it and help it grow. Maybe this was the man God had called to bring it to the next level and restore it for the children? We had to trust he was. Sandy and I had given all we could, both financially and physically, and God knew it. So we accepted his offer.

The Bishop was from Texas, and we decided to drive over and meet him and his wife, on the way home from visiting our family in Florida. As soon as we met them, Sandy and I knew this was the couple we had been praying for. They call that a kindred spirit. Visiting with them a while we found out a little about how God had prepared them over their ministry years.

Let me tell you about him, and you decide for yourself if all his training was just coincidence, or was God working behind the scenes to get them ready?

He began his ministry service in *1988*. I don't know if it was August 8 like us, but I would not be surprised. He became a Program Manager for a Women's Shelter. He added the Open Arms Men's Shelter in 1989. In 2001 he created a Drug Substance Abuse and Spiritual Guidance ministry called the Abstinence Program. In 2002 he created a Food Pantry Program for the community and expanded it to include donating clothes to the homeless. In 2003 he worked with a Child Feeding Program that fed children throughout the city. In 2003 he worked with youth ages thirteen to eighteen every Saturday morning, counseling them with behavioral problems. In 2004 he and his wife became foster parents.

On August 24, 2016, our prayers were finally answered and we turned over the center to those we believe are God's chosen servants to carry it forward. On August 28 we paid off more of the ministry debt. One such debt I had been praying for three years to complete paying off. These folks helped us in a time when there seem to be no way. God will make a way where there seems no way.

On September 10, 2016, they had their first meeting at the Center to begin opening up and restarting the programs God had been doing there all these years.

Praise God for His faithfulness once again.

Conclusion

It's hard to close this book because there are so many more stories I could continue to tell about this magnificent ministry. It suffices to say there will be trials of various kinds that will come into our lives. They never end. There is no one time cure all answer I can give you. I can tell you if you are following Jesus you will look back and see the triumphs will far outnumber those trails that come along life's way. Many of the trials will lead you to triumphs and blessings.

There is a handbook you can follow, and I would pick one up if you don't have one. There is Someone that will walk with you through your life. The handbook is the Bible, and the someone is Jesus. He will also send people into your life that will help guide you in His direction for your life. You will know who they are because they will have no personal or ulterior motive in their wanting to help you. They will be led by God, as we are, to do something that He alone has placed in their hearts.

If it were not for the faithful Prayer Partners God sent us all these years, this ministry would not have existed. This book and the first book would never have been written. Many times, we would not have money even for groceries for the week and we would receive a check in the mail that would provide them. Once again I must say Thank You to all those who God has blessed us with as dear friends these many years.

Perhaps the best way to express my thanks to two of those people who were instrumental in guiding me into His service, is to end this book by giving them recognition.

"I believe God has a calling on your life," Pastor Norman Green said to me. "Get out of here," I said. "No, I feel He is calling you into the ministry, pray about it," he said.

We were attending First Assembly of God Church in Burbank, CA. Our first Sunday there, I had passed a little slip of paper up to the Pastor asking if I could sing a song. He graciously agreed and I sang the song "He's Alive." That was the beginning of this marvelous journey.

This church became our home church, and Pastor Green became my pastor, teacher, guide, and friend into a life I could have never imagined possible. He and his wife, Mary, became as family to Sandy, Dominick Jr., and I. Each Sunday, after services, Pastor Green would take Nicky (Dominick Jr.) by the hand and they would, "**Check it out.**" That meant they would walk together and check out all the church doors to make sure they were secure before leaving the church for the night. College Bible Studies were foreign to this actor/entertainer, but with Pastor Green's help, they became easy. My first Ministerial License was with the Assemblies of God, and the rest is history.

I challenge you to take a step of faith and see your Trials turned into Triumphs with the only One who can make that happen. It is hard to believe twenty-eight years have passed since we took the challenge Jesus gave to the rich young ruler in the Bible. **Matthew 19:6-22**. He refused it, but we accepted. The joys of writing these two books have been great reminders to me of our Lord's faithfulness to those who trust, delight, and commit their lives to Him. **Psalm 37: 3-5**

So in closing I want to say, take a hold of the hand that has been reaching out to you from your very beginnings and "**Check it out**."

Pastor Norman Green, Nick, Sandy, and Mary
(Photo taken by Steven Kulzer)

Acknowledgments:

Cover Photo provided by Blue Cross/Blue Shield Angel Award Louisiana

Back Cover Photo provided by Life Touch Portraits

Pastor Norman Green, Nick, Sandy, and Mary (Photo provided by Steven Kulzer)

All other photos are personal photos of Nick Farone

Thanks to our friend Barbara Jacobson for her Photo Editing